The
EVERYDAY PARENTING
TOOLKIT

ALSO BY ALAN E. KAZDIN, PH.D.

The Kazdin Method for Parenting the Defiant Child

The
Everyday Parenting Toolkit

THE KAZDIN METHOD FOR EASY, STEP-BY-STEP, LASTING CHANGE FOR YOU AND YOUR CHILD

Alan E. Kazdin, Ph.D.

WITH CARLO ROTELLA

HARPER

An Imprint of HarperCollins*Publishers*
Boston • New York

First HarperCollins edition 2014

Copyright © 2013 by Alan E. Kazdin and Carlo Rotella

www.harpercollins.com

Library of Congress Cataloging-in-Publication Data
Kazdin, Alan E.
Everyday parenting toolkit : the Kazdin method for easy, step-by-step,
lasting change for you and your child / Alan E. Kazdin.
p. cm.
ISBN 978-0-547-98554-1 ISBN 978-0-544-22782-8 (pbk.)
1. Child rearing. 2. Parenting. I. Title.
HQ769 .K345 2013
649'.64—dc23
[B]
2012537349

Printed in the United States of America

23 24 25 26 27 LBC 13 12 11 10 9

Contents

Acknowledgments

We would like to thank our children for all they have taught us, and we would like to thank the many parents we have encountered whose dedication to child rearing has been an inspiration and an example.

Introduction

A lot of people associate the word *science* with cold, remote abstractions, the opposite of your relationship to your kids. But scientists who investigate parenting and child rearing are finding out all kinds of things that can make family life not only easier for parents and children but also warmer, closer, and happier. In psychology and related fields, researchers are studying everything from the most effective way to ask your child to do something (the way that's most likely to lead to the child doing it) to how and why parents punish so much even though it doesn't work very well. The body of good research produced by these scientists grows more robust and useful every day. Their findings confirm some instinctive parental habits. For instance, research on the effects of comforting touch is telling us more and more about how good for your kids it is, not just psychologically but biologically, to be hugged by you. When you follow the urge to hug your child frequently, the likely good effects include not only reducing stress and promoting bonding and attachment but also strengthening the child's immune system. The research also shows why other ingrained parental habits make life only more difficult for adults and children alike. Take nagging, for example. We (I say "we" because I'm a parent, too) tend to act as if repeatedly reminding a child to do something makes the child more likely to do it, but the science clearly shows that the opposite is true: more reminders equals less chance of compliance.

There's good science out there, and parents need it more than ever. They're pulled in more directions than ever before and get less help than ever from other adults. They have less time with their families because of the normalizing of the two-career couple (or, for that matter, the three-job or four-job couple) and the technology-assisted expansion of work to fill even the smallest gaps in the day, so that parents are never beyond the reach of e-mails or text messages that draw them away from family time and back to work. There are also more single parents than ever before: in the United States, 41 percent of births are to an unmarried parent, and many parents are raising kids largely alone because of divorce. More grandparents have primary responsibility for rearing children, and there are more blended families in which different approaches to raising children can come into conflict. And, crucially, parents are increasingly isolated, cut off from the support systems and sources of advice that have traditionally helped with child rearing, such as neighbors and grandparents.

That all translates into more and different kinds of stress on parents. You try mightily not to pass this stress on to your kids, but its effects can sneak up on you. Take, for example, that typical twenty-first-century mini-storm in which you get an emergency text message from the office and then your toddler melts down or your preteen goes into attitude overdrive. "Just my luck," you may think. "This is the last thing I need right now." It's natural to think of the simultaneous onset of work-related and family-related crises as a coincidence — bad parental luck — but they're often deeply connected. A number of studies show in detail how stressors on parents modify how they interact with their children, often in ways that increase noncompliance. When a parent is under stress, especially when stress is made worse by isolation, the effects can be measured by changes in tone of voice, the quality of prompts to children, patience, and the ability to pay attention to a child — all of which can make a child more difficult to manage. Just a little more edge in your voice, just a little more or less slack in reaction time can make the difference between a child doing what's asked of him and pitching a fit. And, of course, a difficult child is another stressor, which in turn stretches and isolates the parent even further, and the whole cycle goes around faster and faster.

Feeling on their own and in need of support, parents increasingly turn to our age's principal substitute for community and extended family: the Internet. Studies show (yes, somebody's studying this) that parents go online for advice more than they go to their own parents or to others who are raising children of the same age. And there is indeed some useful information to be had online if you know where to look. The problem is that much of it is not presented in a way to make it useful to nonscientists, and, more important, even the best advice is buried in an electronic infinity of bad advice, bad science or anti-science, and confident admonitions to do things that won't work and may well make your life worse: talking your child's tantrums to death, for instance, or whupping the badness out of your child, or using time out for hours until your child learns her lesson. It can be difficult to tell the good advice apart from the bad, especially when you're not an expert and in a hurry. And you probably *are* in a hurry, especially these days.

I direct the Yale Parenting Center, a service for families at Yale University that works with parents who want help with their children. Families in nearby cities and states come to the center for face-to-face sessions, and through our online setup we work with others from across the nation and in other countries. We see all kinds of kids and parents, all sorts of situations and problems, including some very extreme ones, but typically we focus on families that are dealing with the common challenges of child rearing. Sometimes these parents need a little help to get them through a rough patch, a child's particularly challenging developmental stage, or a sticky situation—of which we've seen all kinds, including a lot of out-of-control tantrums, teasing and fighting among siblings, children who won't do homework or practice an instrument, and every kind of teen attitude you can imagine. And sometimes they don't have a pressing problem at all, and they're just looking for assistance with normal day-to-day parenting, like managing multiple kids' schedules or preparing for a fast-approaching transition to adolescence.

We've seen thousands of children at the Yale Parenting Center, from toddlers to teens. But it's important to make clear that the methods I'm presenting to you in this book are not just the product of my own experience. They're drawn from the findings of science, which means that they're drawn from the experiences of a much larger pool—thousands of scientists and all the many, many people they have studied. These experiences have been systematically collected and analyzed, and that analysis is continuously tested and refined. Science does not have all the answers, of course, but it's our best means of accumulating information and improving knowledge over time. The scientific method has allowed us to make gradual progress to the point that we can control diseases that used to be incurable; it's why we can send a spaceship to Mars, which used to be a science-fiction fantasy; and it's why we can now effectively treat formerly intractable afflictions like anxiety and depression. This book is based on what scientists in psychology and allied fields—not just me, but a whole profession's worth of fellow investigators—have learned that can help you do everything from toilet training your child to dealing with typical teen issues like enforcing curfews and managing greater independence.

The parents I meet need a guide that bridges the gap to the best science and makes it immediately available to them in the most practical ways. So that's what I set out to do in this book. I've already written a book for parents that focuses on the particular challenges of dealing with defiant and oppositional children (*The Kazdin Method for Parenting the Defiant Child*); this book, by contrast, is intended for parents who are dealing with the kinds of everyday challenges that come up in most households. It brings the most useful results of the research on parenting and child development to you in the form of concrete tools and strategies for your home, illustrates their applicability with everyday examples, provides guidelines on how to use the tools to address fresh situations that may come up in your household, and focuses on routine everyday life behaviors that are challenges to most parents most of the time. This is a parenting handbook for daily life, in other words, at a time when many parents feel, for good reason, that they need more guidance than ever before.

Think of this book as a how-to manual that not only offers effective solutions to common parenting problems but also shows you how to break down and deal with the bewilderingly infinite variety of challenges that come up as you raise your children. It's a book you can turn to when dealing with typical concerns ranging from specific behavior problems to more general matters that transcend the label of behavior, like attitude or character. It will help you work on a concrete issue, such as toilet training or brushing teeth, teaching a child to accept "no" without a tantrum, or smoothing out a conflict-ridden after-school or curfew routine. It will show you how to help your child take more responsibility for doing homework, practicing an instrument, doing chores, or coming home on time. And it will offer ways to help a child develop interests and qualities like respect for others, honesty, good friendships, or altruism. Parents aren't concerned only with behavior, of course; they're urgently interested in their children's character and developing attitude toward the world. But those larger traits will inevitably be expressed as behavior—an honest child will tell the truth; a generous child will perform acts of generosity. By building those behaviors we also work on developing the broader qualities associated with them.

I'll offer plenty of examples, but I won't try to go through all imaginable possibilities case by case. I think it's vitally important to show you a few basic, flexible principles that you can adapt and apply on your own to the limitless variety of situations that come up in the course of regular family life. These basic principles aren't abstractions (of the unobjectionable-but-vague "be firm but fair" variety the parenting literature abounds in); rather, they're specific tools with specific uses, simple enough to master quickly but adaptable to deal with the most complex family situations.

Let's say, for instance, that your twelve-year-old is dragging her heels on weekday mornings and your five-year-old turns every trip to the supermarket into a tragic opera. You'd really like to fix these problems now, and you don't want to embark on some extended personal odyssey of discovery to get to the solutions. So, you check this book—not because it devotes a separate chapter each to morning routines and trips to the supermarket but because a quick look will allow you to review some basic and extremely handy principles. In each case, you know what you don't want the child to do, but have you translated your wishes into a clearly defined *behavior* you do want and can explain to your child? Now, how do you set up the behavior with effective *antecedents* to increase the chances of success? Do you have the *consequences* lined up to reinforce the right behavior, lock it in, and turn it into a habit?

The core of this book is the ABCs: A for antecedents, which is everything that happens before your child does (or doesn't do) what you want him to do; B for behaviors; and C for consequences, which is what happens after your child does (or doesn't do) what you want. The book brings together research in these three areas—how what happens before, during, and after affects the likelihood that a child will do what parents want her to do. I'll show you how to break down a problem into these three components, and I'll offer you tools to deal with each of them.

The first four chapters introduce you to the ABCs—antecedents, behaviors, and consequences—and how to use them. (It takes four chapters because I devote two to consequences, the most overused and widely misunderstood part of the equation.) Chapter five is about what's going on around the behavior, the more general climate of a household. Often, you can raise your overall chances of success in improving behavior by making a simple adjustment in the routines of family life: the context.

Finally, in chapter six I focus, with examples, on how to put the pieces together. Along the way, as I've said, I'll be sure to show you not only how to use the tools but how to decide which tool you'll reach for in a given situation.

It's important to underscore that the *how* really matters here. Many of the good-behavior techniques I present to you have many variations. That's what makes them adaptable to so many different circumstances. Time out and positive reinforcement, for instance, are used not only with children in household, baby-sitting, camp, pre-school, and school settings, but also with adults in nursing homes, the military, sports training, and many other settings. Parents can take advantage of the great flexibility of these techniques, adapting them to their own needs, but they still have to use them properly. Success can often depend on relatively subtle nuances in how you use the technique. Time out, for example, is a very popular tool in the parental toolkit, but it's usually used improperly. Yes, variations are possible, but there are, in fact, more and less effective ways to use time out, and an understanding of the difference between them begins with an understanding of what time out really means: a brief break from any reinforcing events of any kind. And yet adults often do things that undermine the effectiveness of time out: dragging the child to a time-out spot and forcibly keeping her there (which is stimulation, and the wrong kind of stimulation at that); letting the time out go on too long (only the first minute is necessary for changing behavior; everything after that is either neutral in effect or, after about ten minutes, counterproductive); ordering the child to spend the time out contemplating and repenting his sins (when in fact the point of time out is to do nothing at all).

You may recognize some or many of the techniques I discuss. Often, a reader will be familiar with a particular tool, but that doesn't mean it's been used properly in the past. You may have said "Good job!" to your child until it makes you ill to hear yourself say it, but I can show you what the science says about how to praise more effectively—and, as a bonus, you can offer a lot less of it and still get better results.

In that connection, it's important to emphasize that this book isn't another version of a reward program. If you know the parenting literature or have searched online for help with parenting, you may be overly familiar with sticker charts and the like. You may even have tried such programs, with mixed success at best. A successful program requires all three components: As, Bs, and Cs. Point programs—also known as sticker charts—show up a few times in this book, but always as a minor part of a more comprehensive approach. As they're typically used, sticker charts concentrate all of a parent's effort on the Cs, the consequences, with little attention to antecedents or shaping the desired behavior as it develops. But that's like training a pilot only how to land a plane, not how to take off and fly in all kinds of weather. You have to build a behavior gradually and encourage it to occur in circumstances that make success more likely, and you can't do it all with consequences. That explains why consequence-only programs for improving children's behavior, including some very popular ones, don't work very well. For instance, some families, schools, and even fast-food chains offer incentives for children who get good grades, but that's throwing consequences at long-term outcomes, which is usually doomed to fail. If you want to teach someone to play the piano, you don't save up all rewards until the budding musician can play a Beethoven concerto; you shape interim processes like learning scales, practicing regularly, and so on.

So the *how* (how you use the tools) matters as much as the *what* (the tools themselves). You have to use the tools properly, especially when you're just starting to work on building up a new behavior, getting it to occur frequently, and locking it in with the most effective consequences. But you don't have to be perfect. Less-than-perfect applications of the techniques in this book will still be very likely to improve your child's behavior. (And, because human beings and not robots are involved, a much greater likelihood of success is all one can responsibly claim for these methods. The research shows that they work most of the time on most people, and at the Yale Parenting Center we see lots of families whose experience confirms that finding.)

And there's no need to change your life to use every single one of the techniques I offer you in every possible situation. I'm not proselytizing here. If you're satisfied with your child's behavior in a given area — he goes to bed on time and without any problem, she practices the piano without too much fuss — you don't need to consult this book about it. Sometimes you just don't need to use a tool; if you can open jars of food or remove screws and nails from the wall with your bare hands, leave the tools in the box. But sometimes you really need a tool. If you keep running into the same conflict at the same flash point — meals, screen time, clothing, manners, cell phone, attitude, whatever it is — and you're sick of lecturing, threatening, wheedling, and punishing, you can make life less stressful for all by reaching for one or more of the tools in the kit presented by this book, and using it properly.

The
EVERYDAY PARENTING
TOOLKIT

1

Laying the Groundwork for Good Behavior
A for Antecedents

Antecedents are everything that happens immediately before a behavior—how you address your child, what the child is doing at the time, even the look on your face. Want your child to go to bed on time? To take a bath or do a chore? To tell you where she's going after school? To listen better or be more physically active? What happens before each of these behaviors, or before the moment you want it to happen, greatly affects the likelihood that the behavior will occur. Temperaments and family situations do vary, and different children will be more or less oppositional or cooperative (as any parent with more than one child will tell you), but it's still true that the way you use antecedents can influence a child to do what you wish . . . or adamantly refuse to do it.

Antecedents influence all kinds of behavior in everyday life. A wave from a friend is an antecedent; when you walk over and say hello, that's the behavior cued by the wave; and the pleasure of human contact is the consequence. A warning not to eat spoiled food is an antecedent, too, and it's intended to lead to a certain behavior: eating only food that's safe to eat. If you ignore that antecedent and scarf down mold-covered lunchmeat, you're putting yourself in line for the memorably negative consequence of painful and messy stomach trouble.

When we set out to use antecedents consciously, we do it because we're confident that a certain antecedent has an influence on what happens next. So, one person invited out to a fancy dinner might starve himself all day to gear up to take maximum advantage of the opportunity, but another might eat a snack before the dinner to improve her chances of exercising moderation and not overeating when faced with all that fabulous food. In both cases, the dinner guest consciously does something before arriving that will have an effect on how he or she behaves at the meal.

But the effect of antecedents is not always so obvious. Often, in fact, that effect happens at a level well below our own conscious sense of what we're up to. For example, there's a fascinating area of research in psychology called "priming," which mostly consists of presenting cues to people and then having them engage in some seemingly unrelated activity, like solving a logic problem or arranging a list of words in alphabetical order. Participants in the experiments are not aware of the relationship between the priming cue and the activity they then do, and yet there's a measurable effect on their behavior. Showing test participants a briefcase—seemingly incidentally—before asking them to complete a task made them more competitive, but a glimpse of a backpack made them more cooperative with others. The smell of all-purpose cleaner made them neater. Participants who were given a warm cup of coffee to hold tended to see the personalities of people they encountered during the study as a little more "warm," emotionally, than did participants who didn't hold a cup of coffee. When asked what made them feel more competitive or neat-minded, or why they felt that the stranger they encountered had a warm personality, they couldn't identify the priming influence as a cue. The research on priming should remind us that we're often unaware of how antecedents have a strong effect on our thoughts, feelings, and actions. But the fact that we're often unaware of that effect doesn't detract from their power.

When it comes to parenting, the first thing to bear in mind is that most of us rely too heavily on consequences—punishments, especially, but also rewards—when we're trying to change a child's behavior or mindset. It's natural to fixate on the behaviors or attitudes we don't want and then react to them with reprimands or promises of big rewards to try to get rid of them, neither of which works very well. The human brain is actually hard-wired to respond to negative stimuli, so parents seeking to change their children's behavior have to push back against their own human tendency to be better at noticing and reacting to negative than to positive things.

You will have more success, and life will be easier for you and for your children, if you take more advantage of the power of antecedents. There's a great deal you can do in advance that will make it very likely that the behavior you want will happen when you want it to, whether what you're after is something very specific, like doing homework, or something more general, like listening to you more attentively or speaking respectfully or being more motivated to get off the couch.

This means that you have to know what behaviors you would like, and when you want them. When you have an idea of what you're looking for, it's easier to use antecedents to make it happen. That also gets you out of the habit of just noticing what you don't want, and unwittingly reinforcing it with your exasperated attention. I'll have more to say about all that in the next chapter, which concentrates on the behavior itself. For now, let's stick to antecedents.

Your antecedents toolkit

Let's start with some common types of antecedents. I'll go through them one by one. What we're doing here is putting some equipment in your toolkit—ways to set up the behavior you want.

Prompts are antecedents that directly instruct a specific behavior, such as "Please pick up the clothes on your floor now." They can be verbal instructions, written or physical cues (a note on the refrigerator door, a list of things to do, colored strips of tape on the fingerboard of a child's violin to guide the placement of his fingers), gestures (waving to someone to come in or go out), physical guidance (putting a child's hands in the proper position on a musical instrument or a tool), or modeling (demonstrating how to hold a fork or jump rope). Each type of prompt can be used alone or in combination, and each is directed toward promoting a desired response by conveying what it is and, sometimes, how to do it.

It's natural to favor one type of prompt. Typical family life, for instance, seems to feature a great deal of verbal instruction in the form of shouting from room to room, which doesn't produce much in the way of desired behaviors. (The content of the shouted statement is equivalent to a prompt—"Come in here and clean up this mess you made!"—but the delivery in the form of a shout from a distance will undermine the request and is more likely to lead to noncompliance.) But combining different kinds of prompts is much more effective. If you tell your child to clean her room, that might work, but it will be more effective, especially when you're just beginning to try to establish the behavior as a habit, if you tell her what you want and then say, "Let's go start it together," and then go to her room with her and model the behavior (pick up one piece of clothing off the floor and put it in the laundry bag). Or you could try taking turns as a prompt: I do one, you do one.

Many parents have an almost instinctive resistance to "I do one, you do one" and other such strategies. Understandably, they want their child to be independent, and they fear that helping him do every little task will not teach him to do things on his own. But that's a misplaced worry. It's efficient and effective to be close by at first and to help a lot early in training, because initiating behavior and getting the early steps going are the most difficult part. Firming up the habit later on is relatively easy. As more of the behavior occurs (more cleaning up on her own, more homework time), it works well for a parent to stop offering prompts and back off.

Fading refers to the gradual removal of a prompt. If you abruptly remove a prompt too early in training, you may be interfering with the establishing of a habit. But if your child is consistently doing the behavior when you prompt her to, you can begin to reduce and finally omit the prompt. For example, teaching someone how to serve in tennis or how to play the piano may include reminders (prompts) regarding how to hold the racket or how to place fingers on the keys. As the beginner learns, the nature of the prompt may change—from "Hold your fingers like this" (with the teacher modeling the position) to just saying the word *fingers* without any other statement or modeling. Also, you can provide prompts less frequently. The correct behaviors are reinforced without reminders, and soon these behaviors do not need to be prompted at all, or only very rarely. Finally, the behavior is reinforced without prompts.

If you are going to use just a verbal prompt, it helps to remember that the more concrete and specific the statement, the better. "Please bring me the phone" is much better than "Could you bring me the phone?" (an open-ended question that naturally leads a child to think, "Yes, I am capable of bringing you the phone," but not necessarily to bring you the phone right now) or just "Bring me the phone," a command that eliminates all possibility of choice, with bad effects I will get to in a minute. Both the open-ended question and the imperious command are less effective than making a polite and specific request. Similarly, "Fix your shoes! You're nine years old!" is very unclear and open-ended; "Please tie your shoelaces" is much more likely to produce the results you want.

As you can probably tell, the "please" matters a great deal—both because it conveys a sense of choice to a child and because it serves to control your own tone. It's harder to yell and speak harshly when you begin with "please." Choice, a warm tone, and politeness all help to produce the results you want, as I'll explain when I tell you about other sorts of antecedents.

First, though, one story about the importance of tone and "please" as antecedents. One of the mothers who came to the Yale Parenting Center for help complained that her nine-year-old daughter, Rena, never listened to her when she asked her to start homework, practice her flute, or help with setting or clearing the table. I asked the mother to pretend I was the child to see how she asked Rena to do something. The mother made very clear statements about what to do: "Go to your room and start practicing your flute." The content of the prompt was perfect in clarity. But the tone was a little harsh and she made no effort to soften the request, which therefore felt more like an order. The mother's natural tone of voice sounded harsh to begin with, even when she was just talking about something with me or with the staff at the Parenting Center, and when she spoke to her daughter, it was even a bit harsher.

There is more to getting compliance from a child than tone of voice and presentation, but a harsh tone can all by itself lead to non-compliance. We had the mother practice putting "please" in front of her requests. We asked her to smile a little, too. The "please" and the smile helped make the request much less harsh—they at once controlled how the mother made the statement (more sweetly) and in the process raised the likelihood that the child would comply. (Try it yourself. Even if the content of a command is stern, it sounds gentler if you smile and say "please" while issuing it.) We also had the mother practice going over to her daughter and speaking more softly. So the full package was to say "please," smile, and go closer to the child so Rena's mother could speak more softly and still be heard. Rena almost instantly began to comply more often with her mother's requests and virtually stopped arguing and talking back, which had been a problem before.

Note that we didn't ask Rena's mother to be any more lenient or to change her policies at all. We just helped her make a couple of slight changes in the tone of her antecedents.

Setting events influence a behavior without offering a direct, narrowly focused prompt. They set the stage for a behavior. For instance, reading to a young child to help him wind down before bedtime will increase the chances of a smooth transition to sleep. Setting events can be broad in scope or very specific, and they're used throughout everyday life. The cinnamon cookie smell wafting through the house on display by a realtor or the soft music one hears when boarding an airplane are setting events for desired outcomes: making an offer on a house, taking your seat calmly. Parents arguing before school can be a setting event for their child being noncompliant at school and getting into trouble. We can break down setting events further into whether they make a behavior more or less likely to occur.

Dress codes in schools are a classic setting event intended to promote disciplined and orderly behavior. Dress codes in restaurants, similarly, don't just give the proprietors an excuse to exclude some people; they're also intended to increase the likelihood that dressed-up customers will behave courteously. Giving a child a good-natured challenge ("I bet you can't do this") is often an effective setting event, because it helps motivate the child to try a behavior, increasing the likelihood that it will happen. I know of no generally accepted scientific explanation for exactly why challenges work so well, but the research does suggest some possibilities. It shows us that competition is a terrific motivator, and it's possible that a challenge sets up an implied competition with some standard, like a runner testing himself against the clock, or with a peer group. That's why it can help if you add to the challenge something like "It's OK if you can't do it now, because it's really hard for a kid your age. But maybe when you're older . . ."

A setting event can also make a behavior *less* likely to happen. Eating a big meal before you go to the supermarket decreases the chances that you'll buy a lot of food there. Some convenience store owners pipe classical music out to the parking lot to decrease the likelihood that teenagers will choose to loiter near the store. And, as Rena's mother learned, ordering a child to do something with a drill sergeant tone makes it less likely that the child will do it. "You get over here right this second!" is a prompt, but the harsh tone and stern facial expression with which a parent delivers that prompt also constitute a setting event that makes it less likely that the child will, in fact, get over there right then.

If there's even a whiff of coercion in a command—and in this example there's much more than a whiff, since the child is given no glimmer of choice in the matter—the child is less likely to comply. One interpretation of why that's so is that being coerced even a little leads a child to anticipate consequences he's likely to regret. That is, the "or else" in the implied "do it, or else" is a consequence, and that shades the child's reaction to the "do it" part. People in general are risk-averse, and the child responds to someone trying to force him to do X with the conviction that X is not something the child would otherwise do and therefore might have some undesirable effects for him. A second interpretation is that being told to do something is mildly aversive and leads to escape behavior. One escape behavior is not to do what you're being told to do; another is leaving the situation. Force, or the threat of it, is aversive and invokes a reaction.

With almost any message, how it's delivered can dictate whether you increase or decrease the chances of a certain behavior. For example, hotels want guests to reuse their towels, which conserves energy and saves money. The usual request is something like "Help save the environment and reuse your towels." That purely rational approach, based on a belief that everyone would reuse towels if they just understood how important it is, doesn't work very well. Understanding is a pretty poor motivator to comply with a request: people who smoke understand that it's bad for them, but they do it anyway. But if the hotel adds to the message some statement about other guests reusing their towels, it creates the impression that reusing towels is a social norm, which is a stronger motivator for compliance and thereby makes conservation much more likely to occur. So the message should say something like "Three out of every four people who stay in this room have reused their towels" and *then* make the request. The information that others are doing it is a setting event that greatly increases the likelihood of the guest engaging in the desired behavior.

As a parent, saying to your four-year-old, "Hey, 75 percent of other four-year-olds brush their teeth" isn't going to work. But you *can* say something like "You don't have to brush your teeth now"—or, during toilet training, "You don't have to use the toilet now"—"because you'll be able to do it when you are a bigger boy." Invoking the "bigger boy" is a way of saying that all big boys brush their teeth, so you're offering a social norm by saying that many people do it, *and* phrasing it as a challenge, *and* you're offering choice, all of which increase the chances of success.

Here's a situation I encountered at the Parenting Center that could be addressed by concentrating on setting events. I was working with a family of four that included mother, father, a seven-year-old girl, and a three-year-old boy named Max. The daughter brushed her teeth with no problem, but Mom and Dad could not get Max to brush his teeth on a regular basis. Often the parents—almost always the mother—would take Max to the bathroom and stand there to watch him brush his teeth. There was usually a fight, and often the mother "won" by getting Max to put the toothpaste on the brush and brush for just a few seconds. Then the argument would shift, predictably, to whether or not a few seconds "counted" as tooth brushing. Mom, who was normally a pretty easygoing person, found herself saying things like "Your teeth are all going to rot in your head and people will say, 'Who's that pathetic old toothless man?' and I'll say, 'Oh, he's not an old man; that's my son, Max, and he never brushed his teeth properly.'" She also found herself comparing Max unfavorably to his sister: "Your sister brushed her teeth every night with no problem when she was your age. What's wrong with you?" Comparing a child to a sibling like this usually lowers, rather than raises, your chances of getting the behavior you want, because it compares him to only one other person, as opposed to social norming (as the hotel strategy is called), which implies that many, many people pretty much like him carry out the behavior. Also, the comparisons will build Max's resentment toward his sister, which could turn into a significant distraction and lead him to avoid his parents a little more. So the comparisons decreased the parents' chances of getting tooth brushing from Max on a regular basis.

Once in a while the mother would take the brush from Max and start brushing his teeth herself, but this required a little force and the situation deteriorated from there: Max cried, the frustrated mother often brushed vengefully, meltdowns ensued. As often as not Mom just let it go, not even bothering to tell Max to brush his teeth, since this drama over tooth brushing would interfere with a peaceful bedtime, and she wasn't willing to risk it. Better a well-rested child with bad oral hygiene, she figured, than a child who's both sleep-deprived *and* rotten-toothed.

We asked the mother to practice delivering antecedents in a different way. We asked her to walk Max to the bathroom and say, in a calm and even nonchalant way, "I would like you to brush your teeth. Most children who are four or five years old brush their teeth. If you don't want to or can't do it, that's OK. Maybe just rinse your mouth with a mouthful of water." So now she's using social norming by telling him that most children his age and older do it; she's offering an implicit but good-natured challenge by including "if you don't want to or can't do it"; she's offering a choice by telling him he doesn't have to do it; and she's getting rid of her own tone of desperation and of anticipating the brushing battle, both of which decreased the likelihood of getting any tooth brushing out of Max. (And, on the behavior side, which we'll get to in the next chapter, having Max rinse out his mouth is a good start toward shaping the full behavior she wants, and she's also using what's called "response priming" by taking Max to the bathroom, the first step toward brushing his teeth, without demanding the whole sequence every time.)

So they tried a few nights of the new approach. At first, Max washed out his mouth but didn't brush. The mother reported being able to stay low-key, nonchalant. The nights were pleasant—a little rinse of the mouth and then off to bed, with no scenes. On the fourth night, he said he would like to try brushing his teeth. The mother did not jump up and down (she understood that desperation could turn off the behavior) but said that was "nice" and asked if he wanted her to come in with him. He said no, brushed his teeth, and Mom walked him to bed. His breath smelled like fresh toothpaste and she commented how great that smelled and what a big boy he was to brush his own teeth—just like Mom and Dad did. She was impressed with the changes in the child; we were impressed with her careful practice of the antecedents with us and then her execution on the battlefield—which was, in fact, not a battlefield anymore.

High- and low-probability requests. People do some things more readily than others when requests are made of them. Requests likely to be complied with are referred to as high-probability requests:

"Please come here and hug me," for instance, or "Please help me finish this leftover apple pie." Other requests made by parents, called
low-probability requests, are less likely to be complied with: "Please
do your chores," for instance, or "Please start your homework." The
likelihood of a child complying with a low-probability request can be
greatly increased by preceding it with two or three high-probability
requests—that is, embedding some requests in the context of others
can increase compliance. If you want your child to do twenty minutes
of homework and she tends to resist, you can begin to develop that
behavior by first asking her to do something she'll usually do with no
problem, like feeding the fish or bringing you something. Or take her
to the store and ask her to please go get a specific item that she likes
and put it in the shopping cart. If you start with those high-probability requests and then go to the low-probability request, "Now
please get started on your homework," it's more likely to succeed.
You might expect that a child has a limited capacity for doing what
she's told, a capacity you don't want to waste by piling up trivial
requests to do things, but the research tells us the opposite: there's a
kind of behavioral momentum, a tendency for compliance to persist,
and you can get it going with a series of high-probability requests.

Here's a good practical example. A team of researchers describe
a case in which the goal was to get a twenty-two-month-old child to
cooperate with a complex medical procedure. The boy had a serious bowel condition that required multiple surgeries, and he had an
intravenous line that had to be cared for by his parents. The little
boy would not keep still. He kicked, he pulled at the sterile line, he
made life difficult for himself and his parents. The low-probability request was to hold still so the medical procedure could be completed.
Getting compliance was achieved by first going through some high-
probability requests: "Touch your head," "Say 'Mom,'" "Blow Mom
a kiss," and *then* "Hold still." The last request, a low-probability request, was much more likely to lead to compliance when preceded by
the first three, all high-probability requests.

And of course, this technique works in the other direction. My
advice to preteens and teens is to use high-probability requests liber-

ally, and not to just start out with "Can I have a second cell phone? How about a car?" The teen who draws on the lessons of this body of research will begin with high-probability requests—"May I kiss your cheek again because you are the best parent ever? Could I set the dinner table and do all of the dishes by myself tonight? I would like another chore so I can do more to help maintain the house"—and *then* tack on the low-probability request here. And it will help to allow parents a feeling of choice (of which more below): "Could I have one of those Italian sports cars for my birthday? Either the bright yellow or red would be fine." OK, I offer the advice to teens with tongue in cheek, but the underlying principle in play is no joke.

And this isn't just about parents and children, of course. During a study of real-life situations in which hostages were taken during a robbery, audio transcripts from three robberies allowed a researcher to break down interactions between the hostage taker and law enforcement agents. Requests made of the hostage taker that were classified as high-probability—likely to be complied with—included "How can we contact your wife?" and "Please spell that name for me." The low-probability requests were the sticking points: "Give up a hostage"; "Go to the door with your hands up." The results showed that the hostage taker was much more likely to comply with a low-probability request if it was preceded by three or more high-probability requests.

Choice. As I mentioned before, choice is an antecedent. If a child feels that he has a choice about whether to do what's asked of him, he's more likely to do it. The choice can be empty or trivial to you, but it's not to him. "Put on a jacket; we're going outside" might be sufficient to get the behavior you want, but "Please put on your jacket or a sweater—it's your choice—and we'll go outside" is much more likely to work. Especially as your child gets older, you want to look for opportunities to give real choices between alternatives that are both acceptable to you. If you're trying to get a reluctant child interested in music lessons but you don't care as much about what specific instrument he plays, you might take him to a music store and let him play around with the instruments, an activity that implies a choice about which instrument to settle on. Once an instrument is chosen, you can offer choice where possible: "You can practice your violin before we eat or right after dinner." As a general rule, lowering the amount of coercion in your lives (the amount of "Because I said so," whether explicitly stated or just implied) will increase overall compliance.

Offering choice can have subtle and unexpected benefits. One of the moms at the Yale Parenting Center was very concerned about the whereabouts of her fourteen-year-old daughter after school, a well-placed concern under almost any circumstances, as unmonitored teens often get into much greater trouble—more sex, alcohol and other substance use, more risky behavior such as driving with older peers—than monitored peers. Added to the usual concerns, Maya was a sexually mature fourteen-year-old, and very attractive. Older boys were pursuing her, and the mother was concerned about sexual activity and alcohol. Maya usually came home from school one to two hours after dismissal. Her mother grilled her. "Where were you? Who were you with? What did you do?" All good questions but, especially if delivered rapid-fire as she came in the door, all setting events for Maya going straight to her room without talking much to her mom.

When the mother came to the Parenting Center and asked for help, we suggested she chat with Maya when they were both calm. We directed the mother to use one of these chats to explain her concern and suggest two ways they could handle her desire to know where Maya was and what she was doing: (1) Maya could use her cell phone to report where she was, or (2) Maya could come home to check in and then go out with her friends. The mother told Maya that either one of these would be fine, or Maya could suggest some other idea, as long as they could both agree on it. She also told Maya that if on any day she did not report in, the next day she would have to come home directly from school and stay there (a consequence). Constructive use of antecedents here included Mom's calm presentation at a time when no argument or nagging was likely to occur, and her presenting Maya with a choice of alternatives or even coming up with a new one.

Unexpectedly, Maya chose *both* of the alternatives her mother had offered. She wanted to call home by 3:15 (school got out at 2:45) or be home by 3:15 — and she wanted to have the option each day. The mother agreed. Even more surprisingly, and it was a very pleasant surprise, on about half the school days over the next few months Maya came home and elected to stay in and chat with her mother rather than going out again.

Which antecedents should you use?

I have covered a variety of antecedents. How to select among them in any given instance? One place to start: it is almost always useful to select both a prompt (a direct way of getting behavior) and a setting event (a more indirect way). These work together well.

On the prompt side, the usual is just to give instructions or make a request. That's fine, but if you have any difficulty in getting the behavior, there are more effective prompts such as doing the task (just a small part) with the child or modeling the task (doing it right before the child does to show what you mean or how it's done).

On the setting event side, think of what can be done to make it easier for the behavior to occur. I mentioned offering a choice if possible, because offering options makes compliance with the request more likely. The usual choice — "You either do this, or else" — isn't much of a choice. Instead, offer real options: "I can help you, or would you rather do it yourself?" or "You can do this now all at once or do a little now and a little later."

Also, think about any setting events that are currently interfering with getting the behaviors you want. Is there anything happening right before your request that may make the child less compliant or responsive? One example of this you may be familiar with: a very young child who is hungry, thirsty, or tired is not likely to be compliant or agreeable. For very young children — and many adults, too—hunger, thirst, and exhaustion are such powerful negative setting events that nothing else is likely to be accomplished until those are resolved. Be on the alert for influences that may be making it more difficult to get the behavior you want.

I also mentioned high-probability requests as a setting event. You may not use this tool very often, but it can be useful. If you think your next request will inevitably be met with resistance, get compliance on some easy ones first. You are building compliance, and that helps produce further compliance. This tool is also good to have in your kit because it conveys the role of momentum. That is, once you get one behavior, you can get onto a sort of behavioral roll. That doesn't mean you will definitely get what you want, but it does increase the likelihood.

Whatever you select, there are a couple of points to keep in mind. Antecedents are extremely useful, but they're the least-well-used tool in everyday parenting. As I have noted before, if all is going well and you are getting the behavior you want and in the way you want, you can keep your tools in the box for another day. But if you want to get some behavior you aren't getting, antecedents are strong aids.

The how

Even if you've got the right tools, success depends heavily on how you use them. Tone of voice, use of the word *please,* subtle prompts (the research shows that how close you are to a child, physically, when you ask for a behavior can make a big difference), and timing can all matter a great deal. The "how" really matters when it comes to antecedents. As I've already discussed, the same words, delivered in different ways, can be more or less likely to lead to a desired behavior.

For example, in a group setting (when other students are present in a class, when there's a brother or sister in the room, and so on) both commands and reprimands are more effective if they are whispered or spoken softly from up close to the child, rather than called out from across the room. Nobody has proven exactly why this is so, but some things we have already talked about probably come to bear on it. Prompts called out from across a room tend to be perceived as harsher because a louder command is more likely to startle a child. Also, loud commands in general are associated more with "startle situations," like fire drills and urgent statements on the order of "Don't cross the street until I get there," all of which necessarily remove any illusion of choice. But a loud prompt isn't an obvious emergency situation like a fire drill, and the removal of choice now acts only to make it less likely that the child will comply. Also, a public request for a certain behavior feels more coercive because there's an implied possibility of shame, which feels like the threat of punishment. Not doing what you ask would then be public defiance on the child's part, which you would feel more obliged to meet with negative consequences. So public commands and reprimands put the child in a corner, so to speak, where she feels the lack of wiggle room. Going up close to her and whispering a prompt in a gentle tone is much more likely to succeed.

One of the most common misuses of antecedents is to up the coercion stakes from the outset with threats, ultimatums, power plays, and arguments from authority ("Because I said so"; "Do it or else"). These antecedents have been proven to promote noncompliance. Give anyone — not just your child but your spouse or coworker — the feeling that he or she must do something, that there is no choice, and you will decrease the chances that the person will comply with this and probably other requests.

Stress, too, has a powerful effect on compliance. It makes antecedents measurably less effective, for instance. If you find it hard to be calm and positive when you first get home from work, build in some unwinding time for yourself before you start asking your children for this behavior or that. Removing the stress from your voice and manner will make it more likely that you'll get somewhere with your requests.

Another common misuse of antecedents is to pour on the prompts at the wrong moment. Picture a tween or teen just returned from school, backpack still over her shoulder, engaging in one-handed texting. When she walks through the door, a parent comes on strong with caring questions: "How was your day? Anything going on at school? How's your homework for today? You forgot your lunch this morning, so what did you eat? What did you do after school?" Each question is fine, and they may all be delivered sweetly, but the barrage of questions before the child has fully transitioned from the peer world to home gives her a mental version of the bends, the affliction that divers suffer when they come up from the depths too quickly for their bodies to adjust to the change in pressure. The onslaught of questions is a setting event for *not* interacting with you. The individual questions are all nicely delivered antecedents for some pleasant parent-child interaction, but the timing is off. Give her some private time first, so that she can choose to make her reentry into the family scene.

A more dramatic version of this scenario can happen when a child of divorced parents comes back to one parent after spending time with the other. If you're on him when he walks in the door—"How was it at your dad's? Was his new girlfriend there? Was that weird for you? Is she nice? Just in rough general terms, what would you estimate as her body mass index?"—each successive question makes it less likely that the two of you will have the interaction you're hoping for. Give him some time to readjust.

Also, it pays to think about the antecedents offered by the general atmosphere of a household. For example, it's perfectly normal for parents to argue once in a while, but arguments and fights between parents, especially if they become routine, are antecedents for disruptive behavior by children. We'll get to this in depth in the chapter on context.

A couple of examples

Let's look at a couple of examples in more detail to show how to pick and use the proper antecedents.

. . .

Getting a young child to bed can emphasize the crucial role of setting events. Bedtime is usually an occasion for lots and lots of prompts, most of them ineffective: each time you order your child to go to bed and stay in bed and he doesn't, the effectiveness of *any* bedtime-related prompt is degraded. And when the prompts don't work, we go, in desperation, straight from antecedents to an overemphasis on dire consequences: "If you don't stay in bed this time, I'm taking away your teddy bear *forever.*" In addition, of course, when you say such dire things your voice becomes agitated and you've removed all illusion of choice, and so you enter into the territory of what's technically called an "abolishing operation"—that is, the wrong kind of setting event, the wrong kind of antecedent.

Instead, look to the right kind of setting events, those conditions around bedtime that make it more likely that it will go smoothly. That means going back at least an hour in advance of bedtime and planning it like the landing of a jet—the wheels-down moment of the child between the covers is just the last of a series of well-rehearsed moves. The winding-down sequence often includes a bath, a story, and a quiet chat with a parent once the child is in bed, and it shouldn't include computer activities, video games, or TV programs that stimulate the child shortly before bedtime.

Controlling the setting events this way, you create a calmer pre-bedtime routine that consists of a series of things you do that increase the likelihood that the behavior will occur. Each winding-down activity increases the likelihood that the next activity will happen without a fuss, building to the desired outcome: the child gets into bed and goes to sleep without going to war over it. All of the sections of our toolkit are available, of course. Parents can praise a child for completing any of the activities in the pre-bed sequence, but consequences like praise take a back seat to antecedents in this example. Antecedents are where the most effective small changes can be made to the routine to get the result you want.

Let's say you want your teenager to tell you where she is and who she's with after school on days when she doesn't come straight home.

Start with the prompt you give her on her way out of the house in the morning: "Please give me a call after school to let me know where you are and that you're all right. I love you, and I feel better when I know you are safe." You're calm, you imply choice by saying "please," you offer affection—those are setting events that make it more likely that she'll do what you ask. And now strengthen the verbal prompt and setting events (calm, choice, affection) with a touch or a kiss, whatever your teen can stand, on the way out.

A prompt is most effective when it comes as close to the behavior as possible, so doing it right before she leaves for school is better than doing it the night before. The same rule applies to space as well as time: the closer you are to your child when you deliver a prompt, the better. In ideal conditions, you get close in both senses. Let's say Grandma comes over and gives your toddler a toy. He runs over to you, wildly excited, to show it to you. You crouch down to his level and say, quietly, "All right, now go say thank you to Grandma." You're close to the child, and you're prompting the behavior right when you want him to do it, while Grandma's standing right there across the living room, ready to be thanked. In less-than-ideal conditions—that is, in normal conditions—when offering a prompt you just try to get as close as you can to the child in space and to the behavior in time.

Or let's say you want your child to do his homework rather than the usual fooling around on Facebook. When he comes home, allow fifteen or twenty minutes of downtime. Ask him to come and keep you company, if he'd like that. You can have a snack together, or ask him to help you with something that he does easily—like, say, updating the operating system on your smartphone.

Allowing some downtime is a setting event for beginning the homework routine smoothly. Remember, as I've already mentioned, the traditional first-thing-through-the-door parental interrogation is a setting event for not interacting with you—and also for not doing any routine activity associated with you, like homework.

Inviting him to keep you company, share a snack, and answer

your questions about your smartphone are all high-probability requests, setting the stage for the moment of truth. Calmly, and with perhaps a slight smile, you say, "Please start your homework now. I will help you get started if you would like." That's a nice prompt—firm, clear, but gentle, and also offering a choice: "If you want me to help you, I will."

So far, these are all antecedents. You're setting up and framing what you want to happen in ways that make it more likely to happen.

Combining

Antecedents can be very effective in their own right, but they also work in concert with tools drawn from the other categories we will discuss. I've spotlighted antecedents in this chapter, but they're also part of the bigger picture.

Let's say your twelve-year-old son and nine-year-old daughter are bickering and you want them to stop. Antecedents can be very useful here. You might take your son aside in a private moment and say, "Please stop all this arguing and name-calling. Let's get you and your sister apart for a while. Come with me to the kitchen and help me get lunch ready." And you can add more: "I know this is not all your fault, but I need you to help me put an end to the bickering. You're now like one of the grownups in this house, and I know you can control yourself better." This takes away implied blame, which is an antecedent for reacting negatively to you. You can apportion blame later, if you need to; for now, you just want to end the arguing in a constructive way. Treating a preteen like an adult is often a setting event for compliance.

Let's say it works. He stops arguing with his sister and starts to walk away with you. That's the behavior you want. So, it's time for the right consequences. You lean over to him and praise him quietly, being specific about what was good about what he did. "That was really great, and very mature of you. I asked you to stop bickering, and you did." A relaxed high-five might be good right here, to reinforce the verbal praise with touch, thereby increasing the likelihood of compliance with your requests in the future.

In the next chapter we'll focus on the second stage of this sequence, the behavior itself. First, though, let's wrap up the discussion of antecedents.

Conclusion

Antecedents come before the behavior. Sometimes they come right before, as when you prompt a child to set the table or wash her hands. Sometimes they come well before, as when you start the winding-down sequence an hour before bedtime.

The most effective antecedents are delivered calmly, without harshness, with "please" and the promise of flexibility in one's request, which implies choice. If that strikes you as the kind of wimpy parenting advice that has led to moral decline in our formerly moral nation, think of it this way: a parent who pours on the harshness and coercion is broadcasting a signal that she's not confident that her commands will be obeyed; a parent who's confident of the outcome can afford to be relaxed about a prompt.

When you are stressed—when you're expecting a tough day at work and you're under a deadline to get out of the house and the zipper broke on your child's only clean pair of jeans—you will lose your cool. That's normal. But realize that your normal reaction will greatly influence your interactions with your child at that moment. You will talk with more desperation, your requests will be more like commands, and, if you're dealing with a small child, you will be just a little rougher in putting his arms through the sleeves of his jacket. You will get more resistance as a result; the change in antecedents will produce opposition. That's normal, too. Your own calm, confident, relaxed assertion of authority is one of the most important antecedents at your disposal—a setting event for success when you're seeking to change your child's behavior or mindset.

Now, some reminders about basic dos and don'ts when using the antecedents I've talked about in this chapter. These are fundamental matters of approach, no matter what kind of antecedent you employ.

Dos
- Be calm.
- Be clear and specific in prompting what you want.
- Bear in mind that tone of voice and facial expression can affect the likelihood of getting the behavior.
- Be near the child and speak softly if you can.
- Put "please" in front of any request because it helps increase the likelihood of compliance.
- Try to use prompts when they are most effective, by offering them right before the behavior you want.
- Give choices when possible because doing so increases the likelihood of compliance.
- Use a range of antecedents. If you usually concentrate on prompts, think a little about setting events. If you're stuck on a low-probability request that your child doesn't often fulfill, try stringing together some high-probability requests in front of it.

Don'ts
- Don't point dramatically or snap your fingers at your child while ordering him to do something.
- Don't use phrases like "because I said so" or "because I am your parent."
- Don't rattle off a given prompt several times within a brief time period. This is nagging, and a lot of good research has confirmed what people who have been nagged already know from experience: nagging doesn't work very well.
- Don't harp on the negative consequences to come if the child doesn't do what you want. This kind of threatening, whether of the "your teeth will all fall out before you're twenty-one if you don't brush them" variety or of the "I will give you such a smack" variety, is remarkably ineffective.
- Don't worry that all these antecedents are just babying the child, cajoling, or making the child dependent on you. Just the

opposite—antecedents are useful in getting exactly the behaviors you want and in getting them to occur consistently later, once the antecedents are a distant memory.

- Don't give in to the urge to go straight to consequences when you're not seeing the behavior you want. You can work wonders with antecedents.

2

What You Want to Change
B for Behaviors

Behavior consists of any action or response you can observe. Talking, walking, tantruming, fighting, helping, cooperating, complying—all are behaviors. Most of what parents want to change or develop in their children qualifies as behavior. Typically, they want to see one of three kinds of change: they want a child to do something she doesn't ordinarily do or has never done or does only once in a while; or they want more of a behavior the child already does (practice the piano longer, read more pages or more advanced books, do homework for more minutes); or they want to develop a sequence of separate tasks that go together but are actually a bunch of different behaviors—like taking care of a dog (food, water, a walk twice a day) or getting ready for school in the morning (getting out of bed, showering, getting dressed, coming downstairs on time to eat and pack a backpack).

But it's important to recognize that as parents we do not want just a pile of behaviors. We often have larger goals in view, like building character and developing personality traits. We want the child to have broad virtues such as honesty, independence, diligence, and kindness, and to be respectful and to express gratitude. We don't want just one honest act, one isolated act of kindness. No, we are hoping to raise a decent, strong person, which adds up to a lot more than just whatever specific behaviors we had time to focus on at home.

As it turns out, the way to develop any of those characteristics is to develop individual examples of it, which of course brings us back to changes in behavior. If you would like your child to be kind, start by helping her make a habit of kind gestures. You can begin with just a couple of them—in the home, say, toward her younger brother—and then extend them outward toward non-family members, strangers, and so on. If you're trying to develop kindness as a general set of behaviors, to raise a child who is kind in many ways and in many different situations, you don't have to develop each different way in which kindness is shown. Once a child learns to engage in kind actions in a few areas of life, other expressions of kindness that you didn't train will increase as well.

Even when we're concentrating on just behavior, we often want chunks of behavior rather than picky little bits of action. You want a child to do his regular chores, for instance. If that includes setting the table and your child is older, you may not have to separately train him where to put the fork, then the knife, then the spoon, then the napkin. Your child may well have seen you set the table many times (you already modeled the behavior for him, which is a strong way to teach it) and may have helped you do it. With other children, especially younger ones, you might indeed have to start by building one piece of behavior at a time—where the fork goes, and so on. We begin with what the child can do, and then build from there. Wherever we start, we're heading to the same place: setting the table as a cluster of behaviors within the larger cluster of doing one's chores. One strength of this approach is that it can be individualized to meet a child where he is, beginning with what the child can do and building from there.

Often, building the characteristics associated with the behavior is as important as or more important than the particular behavior itself. Consistency is a good example. A child might do her homework on Monday and Tuesday but then tail off as the week goes on. Another might practice an instrument for twenty minutes on one day, skip the next, and play for only five minutes on the following day. When consistency becomes a problem, we can focus on and alter consistency itself as if it were a separate behavior. I'll show you how in this chapter.

So while developing specific behaviors often does involve thinking about one concrete action at a time, it does *not* mean that we have to separately train a child to do every single thing we want her eventually to be able to do. We focus on concrete and specific behaviors not only because it's important to us that our child can do them but also because the training carries over to very similar behaviors that we don't have to train. Establishing a particular behavior can be the end in itself ("I just want her to do her homework every day") or a means to a broader end ("I want her to be a responsible and organized person").

Your behaviors toolkit

Unlike in chapter one, when I filled the antecedents toolkit with a variety of antecedents for you to choose from (prompts, setting events, and so on), this time I'll walk you through a process: how to identify the behavior you want and how to work with your child to develop it. You will have some choices about which tools you use to build a behavior (shaping, simulations, jump-starting), but in this chapter we're going to concentrate more on how you work through the *process* of setting goals and then getting the behavior you want.

Setting your goals. To begin with, you need to *specify what you want your child to do.* As odd as it may seem, parents rarely specify to each other or to themselves, let alone to their children, the behaviors they want in their children. They're very clear on what they *don't* want to see. As soon as the child does something annoying, problematic, or disrespectful—lying, refusing to bathe, leaving new clothes strewn on the floor, teasing a sibling, swearing—parents are typically ready to pounce. But they rarely specify what exactly it is that they *do* want. This is the negativity bias, the hard-wired human tendency to respond to negative stimuli that I've already mentioned, in action.

Specifying sounds simple, and it can be. It's merely describing what the behavior you want would look like. Be concrete. "I want my child to be nice" describes a character trait, not a behavior. "I want my child to share toys with his sister and speak politely to her when they watch TV or we eat dinner together" is more useful because it describes behaviors you want and the circumstances in which you want them. At the Yale Parenting Center we help parents specify behaviors in concrete terms by asking them to pass "the stranger test"—that is, to describe the behavior they want to see as if they were speaking to a stranger who had no idea of what their child did or what the behavior would look like. Ask yourself, "What exactly would the behavior I want my child to do look like? What would she say and do, and how would she act?"

This initial step is a very important part of the process. A couple in their late thirties came to the Yale Parenting Center for help with their five-year-old son, Daryl, who was, they said, constantly bullying his seven-year-old sister, Ella. They wanted help in getting him to be nice to her. We always begin by hearing the story as the parents frame it, and Daryl's parents' desire to move from "constantly bullying" to "being nice" oriented us in a general way to the challenge at hand. But we needed details, especially specific behaviors that Daryl did that we could change. The father resisted my request for specifics. Understandably, he felt that Daryl did so many things wrong that we shouldn't limit our efforts to changing just one or two of them. He wanted to get Daryl to be nicer to his sister in all ways, whether or not we could specify them all at the outset.

I explained that we would in fact address the full range of his concerns and general goals, but to do that we needed to focus now on a few behaviors they found especially troublesome. We would specify those, change those, and work on others as needed. There was no need to focus on each and every possible behavior that Daryl would conceivably come up with. Rather, once we changed a handful of key behaviors, probably one to three of those, other behaviors would change along with them. It's like training a child to play the piano,

I told Daryl's father. The child learns to read music and play a song. Then we teach him to play another song. The behavior of reading music and playing can now extend to many other pieces without us having to focus on each piece as if it constituted a completely fresh and new skill. Similarly, we teach a child to be considerate in a few situations (for example, in play with the children next door, in sharing a dessert with a sibling), and then other, similar behaviors come up on their own. When a grandparent gives our child a present, we prompt the child with "What do you say to Grandma?" and the child dutifully says, "Thank you." But if we do our job as parents properly, the behavior carries over into many other situations that we didn't specifically prepare him for. Your child will one day be saying "thank you" to teachers, colleagues, and lots of other people who aren't his grandmother. Being specific allows us to change behavior, and that specific focus is the best way to achieve the general goals. I asked Daryl's parents to just try this approach.

After some chatting, we identified three of Daryl's worst offenses: he would go into his sister's room when she wasn't there and dump toys off her dresser; he would hit the back of her head, mostly to tease rather than hurt her, whenever he walked by close enough to reach her; he made mocking facial expressions at her at the dinner table. The task was to give me a picture of what happened, what things really looked like, what was said, how it sounded, and so on, and the parents did a fine job of specifying. Their imitation of Daryl's dinner-table faces, in particular, conveyed just how deeply annoying he could be.

The parents felt that dumping the toys and hitting caused the most trouble, so we concentrated on those two offenses. We developed a program for Daryl that focused on replacing these behaviors with positive interactions with his sister. Any time he played peacefully, spoke pleasantly, gave her something (handed her a toy, passed the salt at the dinner table), or had any other positive contact with her, the parents praised him for it and awarded him points toward a small prize he could earn (a consequence, which I'll deal with in depth in the next two chapters). We had a program in place for three weeks, and the parents felt there were great changes in the overall tenor of the interactions Daryl had with his sister. We worked on and changed the specific behaviors of dumping toys and hitting the back of his sister's head, but more general changes occurred, too. Daryl did indeed become nicer to his sister, and it began with specifying what his parents wanted him to do.

Identify the positive opposite. It's likely that many of the behaviors you want to change are behaviors you want to decrease and get rid of—like Daryl's assaults on his sister, or a child spending too much time on the computer or cell phone, or whining, or fighting, or sitting around in her room too much. These are all common concerns, and alterable, but in order to address them we have to begin by defining our objective in a different way. Any time you think of a behavior that you want to reduce or eliminate, the first thing to say to yourself (as a prompt to yourself about what you should do next) is "What's the positive opposite?" That is, what exactly is the behavior you want in its place? Describe what it would look like if you were a radio sports announcer describing exactly what a player was doing so that the listening audience would get a clear idea of what you saw.

Positive opposites are the behaviors you want, the ones you develop to take the place of the behaviors you don't want. So if you want less bickering and fighting between siblings, identify the positive opposite behavior: "I want my children to treat each other with respect when they play, ride in the car, or sit at the table together." If you want less whining, reframe your desire as a positive opposite: "I want her to ask me questions just once, in a big-girl voice." Tantrums, which many parents see as intimidatingly difficult to change, are actually often pretty easy to reduce and eliminate. But first you need to define the positive opposite of a tantrum: walking away from a provoking situation, calmly expressing disagreement without yelling or throwing things, and so on.

The case of Daryl and his sister illustrates the use and importance of positive opposites. Daryl's mother and father knew what behaviors were annoying and had to be eliminated to make home life tolerable for Daryl's sister, Ella. We also asked them to specify some concrete actions they would like Daryl to do that would count as interacting nicely with Ella. They came up with a list that included items such as saying anything nice to Ella; playing together in the same room, either cooperatively or separately, while talking nicely; giving something to her (handing her a toy, passing food at the dinner table). The most effective way to eliminate the undesirable or inappropriate behaviors would be to build up these others to replace them, which is what we did. But the first step was to look to positive opposites to properly set our goals.

If the behavior you want is really a cluster of behaviors, which is often the case, *break it down into clear, doable steps.* Sometimes we are working with one behavior that we simply want more of, or want to see more consistently (such as doing homework, playing quietly). But often we want to develop a set of separate behaviors that go together and follow one from another. Getting ready for school is a good example. This is not just one single behavior we want more of—rather, it's a set of behaviors, or even a set of separate clusters of behaviors, that begins with getting out of bed on time, picking out clothes to wear and getting dressed, coming to the breakfast table, getting school materials together, doing any morning chores, and being out the door, presentable and equipped, on time.

When there are several steps or behaviors along the way, it's important to specify each one. Breaking down the sequence, a practice called "task analysis," is a way of proceeding from the general goal (getting ready for school) to a number of small, trainable, and highly concrete behaviors. The purpose of task analysis is twofold: to identify specific behaviors or steps that are required, and to specify the sequence in which these component behaviors are performed. Task analysis can make it a lot easier to develop a complex set of behaviors.

One example of task analysis is training children how to respond if a fire breaks out in their home. Safely escaping from a fire is not one behavior—such as running like hell to the exit, an instinctive response that can be fatal. Rather, a proper evacuation is a complex set of behaviors, codified by firefighters and other experts after a lot of task analysis and testing in simulated and real situations, and the behaviors can vary depending on factors like how far along the fire is, its exact location, and whether smoke is pouring under the door. The behaviors include crawling on the floor to avoid smoke inhalation, touching the door to check how hot it is, deciding whether to crawl out of the room or cover the crack under the door to stop the smoke from entering, and so on. If escaping safely from a fire is the general goal, it has been divided into trainable steps that encompass several different possible scenarios. Using antecedents, behaviors, and consequences, and with repeated practice, experts have come up with a reliable system to teach children how to escape from their home safely.

Daryl's parents did something similar when they broke down being nicer to his sister into a list of behaviors they wanted to see more of—positive opposites of his current bad treatment of his sister—and then picked a couple to begin to build up. "Being nicer" is an abstraction, but when they broke it down into its component elements, they were able to identify specific behaviors they could work on.

How to get the behavior you want

There are three ways to work on building up the behavior you want: shaping and simulations, which are the two main ones, and jump-starting, which has more specialized uses. You choose the one that best fits where your child is right now. If you're seeing just bits and pieces of the behavior you want, you start with shaping. If you're not seeing the behavior in any form, even partial, or it happens so rarely that you wouldn't have enough opportunities to practice it, you start with simulations. If the child has done the behavior many times but doesn't do it often enough or consistently enough, or used to do it more and now does it less, you might go with jump-starting. Whichever approach you choose, you begin the same way: specify the behavior you want to change, identify the positive opposites of any behaviors you want to eliminate, and then choose which method to use in building up the behavior you want.

Shaping is one of the most potent—and typically underused or mis-used—tools for getting the behavior you want. You shape a behavior, gradually developing it and locking it in, by providing rewarding consequences for small portions, components, or approximations of the behavior you want. For example, if we want a child to do an hour of homework, we begin with brief periods, maybe five or ten minutes. If we want the child to engage in a sequence of behaviors, like taking care of all of his daily chores without being reminded, we may begin by focusing on just the first or second behavior in the set. Shaping begins by asking where the child is right now: Does the child *ever* do the behavior you want? Sometimes the answer is "a little bit, once in a while." Sometimes the answer is "never." Does the child do anything now that even begins to approach the goal? If you want one hour of homework, say, then how much does the child do now, and how frequently? We begin where the child is, and we set out to develop a little more of the behavior, or a little more frequency, until we end up at the goal. Shaping is how we get there. There's an important element of consequences to it: you're arranging to see many repetitions of the action you want and provide positive consequences for it. I'll talk more about consequences in the next two chapters, but in this chapter I'll try to stick to the behavior aspect of shaping.

Parents sometimes use shaping without knowing it. For example, when you're trying to develop use of the word *mommy* or *daddy* in an infant, you will usually reinforce any approximation (*ma, da,* or anything close) by smiling, hugging, and praising effusively. At the same time, but usually without thinking about it, you will typically not give the same level of attention to sounds that aren't close to the words you're listening for. Over time, then, you will tend to reinforce sounds and syllables that come closer to the words *mommy* and *daddy*. (And as you sit close to your child and say over and over, "Can you say 'Mama'? Can you say 'Daddy'?" you're effectively using antecedents. Your modeling of the lip movements and repetition of the sounds are excellent prompts. Your enthusiastic smile and close presence are setting events that will keep your child focused, interested, and eager to please. The prompts and setting events will help your child pronounce the words you want to hear.)

Here's a typical example of shaping. A mom complained that her three-and-a-half-year-old son, Anton, absolutely refused to eat any vegetables as part of dinner, with the exception of French fries (if you count them as a vegetable, about which there's some debate). The dinner routine in that home was 100 percent predictable. The mom usually served salad, a meat or pasta dish, and a cooked vegetable. Anton wouldn't touch the salad or the cooked vegetable. Anton's parents lectured him about why he should eat vegetables, and he listened in dignified silence to their various dire predictions of illness and early death, but nothing they said affected his refusal to eat any vegetable other than French fries. Sometimes his mom made French fries separately for him, just to get something vegetable-like into him. She occasionally threatened to withhold dessert or TV if he didn't eat his vegetables, but she soon abandoned this hard-line approach. She also tried to meet him halfway by declaring that it would be fine if he had just a few forkfuls of vegetables, but that didn't work, either.

The bar-lowering move to the standard of "a few forkfuls" was on the right track because it decreased what was required of Anton in a way that was roughly analogous to shaping. But shaping is not merely lowering the bar; it begins with what the individual already does, then gradually steps up the required behavior. Of course, antecedents and consequences also need to be included as part of shaping.

Because Anton did not eat vegetables at all, you might think that this situation called for simulations rather than shaping; remember, I said earlier that simulations are especially useful when you're not seeing the target behavior at all. But in the case of Anton we went with shaping, for three reasons. First, Anton already had key components of the behavior down. Though he was turning up his nose at vegetables, he ate rapidly, using his fork with dexterity. We just had to change some of the foods he placed on that fork. Second, there were opportunities to work on changing behavior each day that a normally occurring, regular meal was served—that is, we had plenty of chances to work on developing the behavior without relying on simulations. Finally, we wanted to use mealtime directly, not a simulation of it, because we could tell that some of the antecedents and consequences routinely being used in the household were making eating vegetables more of a problem. The number of prompts, the tone employed in giving them, the threats, the dire predictions of what happens to people who don't eat their vegetables—it was all making eating vegetables less likely.

We suggested shaping and a point chart, with an adjustment of antecedents to help increase the chances of success. At the beginning of dinner, the mom told Anton that he could leave the vegetables on his plate without eating them (good antecedents: choice, and a reduction of parental desperation). There was a new point program for him based on dinner. He could earn two points that would be placed on his chart (on the refrigerator) if he put some vegetables on his fork and just touched his lips with it. He could then cash in points to get small rewards that mattered to him—ten minutes extra to stay up and play before bedtime, a glow-in-the-dark ball, a special outing to the park with his father, and so on. He did not have to eat the vegetables on his fork, and he could put them right down once they'd touched his lips. The mom, adopting a nonchalant manner that we coached her in, showed him what this would look like. She noted that she did not worry about Anton eating vegetables—he would probably do that when he was older, like most four-year-olds do (more good antecedents: social norming, and a challenge by implying he is not ready or able yet but will be at some future date). Anton practiced once, and the mom praised that and added, "Remember, you do not have to eat the vegetables." On the first night, he picked up some cooked carrots with his fork, brought them to his lips, and then put them down. His dad said, "That was really good!" and his mom said, "You just earned two points!" Then the mom and dad went on with their conversation. When Anton did it again, they gave him a lot of attention again: praise, points, enthusiasm. All the while, the mother and father were, as usual, modeling eating vegetables, a good positive influence, but now they had removed from the dinner routine many of the negatives—lecturing, pressure, cajoling, and moralizing—all setting events that could suppress the behavior they wanted.

After three dinners in which Anton got points by touching the forkful of vegetables to his lips, his parents informed him that now, to get points, he had to taste the vegetable (put a piece on his tongue), and if he swallowed it he would get double points, but of course he didn't have to swallow it. For the first five minutes of dinner, the whole family made a game to see who could get the smallest piece to stay on the fork to taste and swallow. They were laughing about this, and mock-argued about whose piece was really smaller. Anton ate the part on his tongue. The mother had helped this process along by compromising on her usual austere nutritional habits—using more frozen vegetables and seasoning them with some not-so-healthy ingredients that she knew Anton would like.

They then moved to requiring one full bite of vegetables for points. The next step would have been to move to two bites in order to get any points, but by then Anton would eat a few bites of vegetables and leave a little on his plate by the end of the meal, which was about the same as he did for meat, pasta, and other foods. The parents were satisfied. Also, by this time Anton had some vegetable preferences: he asked for more peas with a sauce and mixed vegetables, and he declared himself less fond of cauliflower and Brussels sprouts. The parents ended the program and dropped the topic of vegetables completely, and from that point on Anton reliably ate them—usually all or almost all of the portions of his favorites, and at least some when his mother served other vegetables.

A few key points about shaping are illustrated by this example. First, it's often difficult for parents to shape behavior. We are often distracted by the fact that the child knows the behavior we want and knows how to do it. Yet shaping is based on what the child *does* now—not on what he knows—and how to get him to a higher level of performance. What a child knows and does not do is not all that relevant—to contemplate it just demoralizes us as parents and tempts us to mislabel the child's behavior as manipulative. Second, we don't demand perfection. This is not a standard we hold for our own performance, and it's the enemy of shaping, which begins where the child is and moves forward from there. In the case of Anton, no demand was made that he eat all of the vegetables served or that he even eat vegetables every night. Shaping requires a flexibility that's not always easy to embrace. Parenting seems easier when we can have rules that never change and have no fluidity, but more effective parenting (that is, for building relationships and behaviors) includes choice, compromise, and tiny vacations from some rules (for example, what has to be eaten at dinner, but not safety-related rules).

Simulation: practice under artificial conditions. The main goal of our method is to get the desired behavior to occur and then to have rewarding consequences follow. Done properly, this repeated sequence locks in the behavior as a habit and carries over to new situations.

So the first goal is just to get the behavior to occur so it can be reinforced. Ideally, the behavior occurs in everyday situations. Shaping is one way to get the behavior to happen, but that requires some early steps or small portions of the behavior to be performed so they can be rewarded. Sometimes the behavior doesn't occur even in partial forms that can be used to begin shaping, and that's when simulation becomes most useful.

If the behavior never occurs, or occurs so rarely that training and repeated practice can't take place, we set up artificial conditions to get it to happen. For young children, it's usually a game or "pretend" session in which they can develop and repeat a behavior. For older children, the simulation can be presented as practice or role-playing.

Let's start with what to do if the behavior you want never occurs. At the Yale Parenting Center we encounter situations like this all the time. For example, in one case, a six-year-old girl named Lia had an explosive tantrum any time she didn't get her way or wasn't ready to do something when her parents asked her to. The tantrums were effective in getting her parents to stop making demands, but of course they couldn't stop making some requests and saying no to her at least once in a while. Lia's parents described her tantrums as "explosive," a combination of being wildly upset, hitting her parents, throwing things, throwing herself on the floor, and continuing to cry or scream inconsolably for long stretches. (Often, her parents would unwittingly prolong the tantrum by holding Lia to restrict her movements, or by yelling or threatening in response to her.)

We asked whether there was ever a nonexplosive tantrum. If there were milder tantrums, we could praise those, increase the likelihood of milder tantrums, and shape increasingly milder tantrums on the way to eliminating all tantrums. But no: the parents reported that every one of Lia's tantrums was explosive and way out of proportion to its apparent cause.

Simulations are perfect for this situation because they allow the child to practice the desired behavior under conditions when everyone is calm and when there is virtually no chance of a real tantrum. We went over how to do this with Lia's parents, and then they introduced the task to Lia when she was calm. Her mother said, "I have an idea for a new game I would like to play. This is called the Tantrum Game" (the exact name doesn't matter). "Here's how it works. First, you can earn points in this game." You can see that antecedents are already in play here as part of the simulation. We use the notion of *game* and make this *playful* because these are setting events that increase the likelihood of compliance and getting the exact behavior you have specified to the child. Similarly, the comment that points can be earned serves as a setting event for the child doing what you will request. Delivered calmly, with a smile, in a playful way, a reminder that your child can earn points is very different from parental pressure—desperation, authoritarian commands, no choice. Mentioning the points also puts the enticing cues of rewards right before the behavior and establishes the incentive front and center. This need be done only once or twice early on in the program; we will want to fade the prompts as we go along.

So Lia's mom went on to explain that "this game is just pretend" and that the goal was to see if Lia could have a "good" tantrum. "If you have a good tantrum, you earn tickets that I have here," said the mom, showing Lia a roll of carnival-like tickets, since Lia loved carnivals (but points on a chart posted on the refrigerator would also be fine), "and with these tickets you can earn some great rewards." These rewards were mostly privileges, minor ones that mattered a lot to Lia and weren't a big deal for her parents (staying up ten minutes later, choosing the menu for dinner), plus a very cheap hair ornament or two (Lia really liked arranging her own hair), that kind of thing. The whole apparatus of points and earned rewards is not absolutely necessary—praise works just fine as a reward when delivered correctly (see the next chapter)—but the points help structure the task for everyone and make it much easier for both the child and parent to follow through.

The mom then explained to Lia that in a "good" tantrum she could get upset but she couldn't scream or hit anyone. We had selected these two components of the tantrum to eliminate first, to initiate the process of gradually shaping milder and milder tantrums. For shaping, we do not need or even want a "perfect" tantrum, only a milder-than-usual tantrum. Remember, the key to shaping is to start out keeping the bar low. If the bar is lower than you think it should be, you are doing a good job of resisting the natural impulse to ask for too much behavior too soon.

After the mother had explained the game, she said, "In one minute I'm going to say no to you. This is just pretend, but I'm going to say, 'No, you can't watch TV tonight.' If you say back to me, 'Why not?' in a calm way and without crying or hitting me, you can earn a ticket. Remember, this is just a game: you really can watch TV tonight." (All of these prefatory comments are great antecedents. First, they state exactly what the parent wants [prompts]. Second, the tone of the interaction—calm, playful, in the context of a pretend game [setting events]—is completely altered from the usual one in which tantrums occur, all of which maximizes the likelihood that the child will do the behaviors, will actually enjoy doing them, and is likely to want to practice a couple of times to earn praise or points. Remember, the goal is to get behavior to occur, and to occur repeatedly.)

Then the mom leaned over to Lia, smiled, and whispered prompts to help Lia succeed: "OK, here we go. It's just pretend, and if you have a good tantrum you can get tickets," and she held the tickets up so Lia could see them. (When developing behavior, one wants to have prompts come immediately before the behaviors are to occur, at least initially.) Then she said, in a regular voice, but gently, "You can't watch TV tonight." With all this heavy use of good antecedents, Lia was unlikely to have a tantrum and very likely to earn the tickets plus praise. So they began, and she had a "good" tantrum, milder than usual and mostly play-acted, and the mother provided effusive praise: "I can't believe you had such a great tantrum. You were pretty calm, you kept your hands to yourself, and you didn't throw anything." Then she rubbed Lia's head affectionately and gave her a ticket.

They could have stopped there for the day, but practice opportunities are the key to this approach. We wanted the child to do it all again. The mother gave a new antecedent—a challenge, as I mentioned in the previous chapter. With a playful, mischievous smile on her face, she looked at Lia and said, "I'll bet you can't do two good tantrums in a row. No six-year-old on earth could do that!" As has been the case virtually every time we have used this technique, the child, in this case Lia, said while nodding vigorously, "No, I can do it. I can do two!" The mom replied with playful skepticism, "I don't know—but ohhh-kayyyy"—as if sighingly giving in against her better judgment—"let's try." They repeated the game with a different scenario—telling Lia that she couldn't go to a friend's house—and of course Lia, who had been nicely primed to succeed, won again. Effusive praise and a ticket followed. That could be the end of simulation for that day, with much accomplished.

The program would be repeated the next day, and the next; the child should have many opportunities within a fairly brief time. At the Parenting Center, we recommend at least a couple of such prompted trials per day, but there is no research to support any particular number and we have worked with parents whose schedules restricted them to just one per day. The general rule is: the more practice opportunities and trials in which behavior can occur and be reinforced, the better.

I mentioned that shaping may be part of simulations. We first want the child to have a milder tantrum than usual during the simulation. Shaping here may refer to beginning by omitting just one component—so a good tantrum might be no hitting, or no swearing, depending on the ingredients of the tantrum—and then gradually omitting more. Over the course of shaping, antecedents are used to help move forward: "I'll bet you can't have a tantrum this time with no hitting *and* no swearing, but if you don't hit and don't swear you can earn *two* tickets," and so on.

After the simulations begin, there are likely to be unprompted occasions when the child does not have a tantrum or has a low-magnitude tantrum (a little whining). That is, the simulations also affect behavior in nonsimulated conditions. You should enthusiastically praise these unprompted mild or milder-than-usual tantrums outside of the Tantrum Game the first few times they occur. The effect of this is to greatly increase the likelihood of milder real-life tantrums. Yet the key to getting this behavior is several practice trials in simulated circumstances. In Lia's case, the mom practiced the simulated tantrums for six days in the course of a week—she missed one of the days. Lia got the hang of it, and her pretend tantrums became milder even without shaping. To the mom's shock, Lia had two mild versions of a regular tantrum (nonsimulated), in a grocery store and about going to bed on time. We had practiced for this moment, so the mom was sure to be very effusive: "I can't believe it! We weren't even playing the Tantrum Game and you had such a big-girl tantrum!" (No points are really needed here and praise delivered well will do the trick.)

It took about two weeks to get tantrums in everyday situations down to a tolerable level and frequency, at which point the game ended because Lia's parents felt that tantrums were no longer a big problem. About a month later, Lia had a pretty explosive tantrum—not as bad as her old doozies, but worse than her recent mild ones. The mom suppressed the urge to panic about a relapse and just walked away, so as to not make things worse. The parents attributed the more severe tantrum to the fact that Lia was very tired after their return from an all-day drive. It turned out to be an isolated event, and Lia's parents dealt with it by ignoring it.

I should note that parents are often stunned when we suggest that they praise a tantrum in any form. They want to get rid of tantrums or make them minimal, and so they logically see praise for their child disagreeing with them or making a scene as exactly the wrong approach. It galls them to reward any kind of tantrum, even one that's notably milder than the usual meltdown. This is when I remind them that as parents they often do reward behaviors that are just little approximations of what they want. I've already mentioned the shaping of a very young child's use of the words *mommy* and *daddy*, and there are other common examples. When you're teaching your child how to swing a bat or catch a baseball, you are very tolerant of imperfections along the way and praise mediocre versions of the behavior as part of the process of getting to more skilled versions of it. Teaching your child to ice-skate or to ride a bike involves a lot of practice under fake conditions: holding the child's arms or holding the bike so it cannot possibly tip over. Yes, mild tantrums are different from these examples because no one is calm or having fun and the two parties have competing views about what should happen—so praising a mild tantrum can feel counterintuitive. But forget for a moment that the behavior in question is a tantrum and just think of it as behavior. We have two powerful tools, shaping and simulation, to get the behavior you want, and rewarding a milder tantrum makes perfect sense.

As I said before, simulations are really useful in two types of situations. I've discussed the first, in which the behavior one wants never seems to occur, which makes it hard to shape even faint approximations of it. The second situation is when the circumstances in which the behavior arises do not occur very often and yet you still want the child to be trained. To take a familiar example from well outside the sphere of child rearing, one major goal in training commercial airline pilots is teaching them how to handle emergency situations—many different kinds of emergencies based on all the things that can go wrong with various combinations of mechanical failure, weather, and so on. One cannot shape good pilot responses while passengers are traveling, not only for safety but because the varied types of situations that pilots ought to be trained in don't occur often enough. So a situation needs to be set up in which the pilot can practice the needed behaviors often and in many different situations so that when a real emergency does come up, the behaviors have been well developed and established. So airline pilots work in a machine called a simulator, a realistic version of the cockpit of a commercial airplane, that allows programming of diverse scenarios, even very exotic emergencies, to which the pilot can practice responding.

In child rearing, there are some situations in which the behavior doesn't occur often but you would like your child to have a well-honed, consistent response. Escaping from a home fire (as I mentioned earlier) and what to do in a medical emergency (call 911) are examples. In each situation, you can't wait for a real fire or health emergency to start developing the needed responses.

Another example is a project that was intended to train a dozen six- and seven-year-olds, six boys and six girls, to not play with handguns. A real but disabled handgun was used. The children were trained in simulated conditions in which a trainer practiced and role-played what to do when he encountered a gun. The safe behaviors that were practiced included not touching the gun, immediately leaving the vicinity of the gun, and telling an adult about it. Children practiced along with the trainer. In order to determine if simulation worked, the children were assessed in real situations at home and at school where they spontaneously encountered a gun (disabled) to see what they would do. Children showed the well-practiced safety behaviors without knowing they were being tested. The test was run again five months later and all children continued to show safe reactions to the situation.

You could do something similar to train young children in what to do when they encounter, for example, a bottle of medicine. You know what you don't want them to do: pick up the bottle, get it open, eat or drink the contents. Now, express that as a positive opposite: do not touch the bottle, get away from it, go and tell an adult right away. To build up that set of behaviors, you can create a simulation game in which you put some medicine bottles on the table and your child can earn rewards by responding properly to them. You can teach even a very small child not to touch the bottle and to go get a parent and say some simple alert phrase, like "Bottle, bottle." Have her practice that response, and reward her every time she gets it right. This is a good example for another reason. As parents we are prone to think that if we convey that medicines are dangerous and the children understand us, that will be enough. We all wish this were the case, but (I will repeat this more than once in this book, because it's important) understanding something is not a strong basis for getting behaviors one wants in ourselves or other people.

Jump-starting is less commonly used than shaping and simulation, but in some situations it's the ideal tool. Sometimes the child readily engages in some behavior and has often done so on recent occasions, but the parents want to see more of it, or to see it more consistently. This is a situation in which the child is more than just familiar with the idea of the behavior—the child has actually done it before, and more than once. In such instances, extensive shaping and simulations to get the behavior to occur may not be required. The response merely has to be primed in some way. Jump-starting, more technically known as "response priming," refers to getting the child into early steps in a sequence or chain of responses. Doing the early steps in a sequence increases the probability of performing the rest of the steps.

A father complained to us that his thirteen-year-old son, Oscar, was too sedentary. Oscar liked sports but mostly as something to watch on TV and to reduce to statistics online. The father was especially concerned because he himself was very active and athletic, and so was his wife. Every Sunday afternoon, the father's friends from work (at a software company) would play touch football for a few hours. Other fathers brought their kids, who often played in the games. The games were more fun than competitive, and there was probably as much break time for scarfing soda, beer, and potato products as for playing actual football. The father wanted to get Oscar to come play football with him on Sundays. He said it would be fun, it would be a favor to him, it would be quality time they could spend together. But Oscar always refused. It is fine to begin with reason and appeals, but they are not likely to work, so be prepared to quickly move on to more effective strategies. (Reason and appeals can clarify the behaviors that are wanted, though, so they can still be useful antecedents to a shaping program.)

Think of playing football with all of the guys as the end of a long series of behaviors. Jump-starting begins with the question "Are there early behaviors that can lead to this end behavior?" If so, we wanted to put Oscar in one of the early behaviors and not worry for now about getting all the way to the final one: playing football with the guys. If we could get one of the early behaviors, the likelihood was greatly increased that the later behaviors would follow. We asked how far away the football field was from home—about a five-minute drive. We wanted that information to see if one of our options for Oscar was feasible. We instructed the father before going to play football to ask Oscar to come with him but *not* to play football. We told him to say he just wanted to be with Oscar that day, just to spend the time. (There were other children there and not all played football, and even those who played didn't play all the time.) The father told Oscar that they would be there together at the field, but that there were lots of breaks during any of which he could drive Oscar back home if Oscar didn't like being there. (Choice of staying—great antecedent.) Oscar agreed to go as long as he was not forced to play—another good adjustment in antecedents, removing all hints of parental desperation and pressure, which might well have acted as a setting event for Oscar choosing not to go to the football field.

Oscar went to the field. His father told him to get a soda and burger if he wanted; the game would start up in about twenty minutes. Oscar's dad had asked a couple of his friends to say to Oscar how nice it was to see him, and they did, which made him feel welcome. Also, Oscar was interacting with some of the other children—tossing a football back and forth a little. Just getting Oscar to the field had put him in the early steps of the sequence—and as the early steps in a sequence occur, other behaviors closer to the goal are likely to increase. In this case, Oscar's dad was very obviously happy to have Oscar there, and it became a weekly event. For the first four or five Sundays, Oscar's dad asked nonchalantly (to get rid of any desperate hope that could promote not going), "Would you like to go today?" We asked the father to drop the question once it was clear that Oscar started to automatically get ready to go and that this was now part of the routine.

After a couple of Sundays, Oscar developed some acquaintances and routinely threw the ball around and ate some food. There was no longer a concern about Oscar playing football, but when one of the friends entered the game, Oscar joined in too so they could be on the same team. He began to play sporadically during the Sunday games—but, mainly, Oscar's dad was just glad that he came, got out of the house, and spent some time with him. Oscar played in the games about as much as the other children, and when he wasn't play-ing he was either tossing a football or horsing around with friends and getting physical activity as a bonus.

The most common errors in developing behavior

Shaping sounds easy and not actually that difficult to do, but it is routinely done in such a way that it fails. There are two related er-rors that can make it fail. The first and more common is that par-ents move too quickly when trying to get the final behavior. Shap-ing requires providing consequences for steps along the way. But the steps—what the child can do, the partial and approximate versions of the desired behavior—ought to be pretty consistent before mov-ing on. Parents often move in steps that are too big or move from one step to another too quickly.

If you want your child to play a musical instrument, she begins by learning how to hold the instrument, how it makes sound, how to read music. Shaping can be slow as the child practices individual notes, combinations, scales, chords, and then a song that draws on versions of these. This is a familiar sequence. If you do this with in-correct shaping, where the child practices notes just once or twice, then moves to combinations or chords, then the scales, each practiced only once or twice, you guarantee that the final behavior, playing the song, will sound bad, and you'll be tempted to conclude that shaping doesn't work.

You want your child to do an hour of homework after school each school day. You tell him he must do this because when you were a child that's what you did. The request and the comment about what you did will fail as a way of changing behavior. Now you add ineffective statements number two—"Other kids do their homework. What's your problem?"—and number three: "Don't expect to get into college without doing homework." All of these statements do a fine job of expressing frustration, but they won't succeed in changing behavior. In the homework example, there's no shaping. We jumped straight to sixty minutes and used only prompts (do it!) to get the behavior. First, shape the behavior by requiring just a few minutes (five or ten), and mix in some antecedents, such as you helping for the first few minutes ("Come on, let's do this together; I can help"), which can be faded later. When you've had a few or several days of consistency, move to a slightly longer time, and so on up to the full hour. Praise consistency as you require more and more time. If the teacher or the school is pressuring everyone to get the homework done and you feel that pressure, you may well be tempted to press for the full homework time right away. Chances are you'll get a fight each time, and at the end of two weeks you will have not made progress. Shaping slowly can get you there faster and better.

If the most common error that makes shaping ineffective is trying to move too quickly or via chunks of behavior that are too large, how do you know if you're going too fast or taking too-big steps? The child's behavior is the guide. If she did ten minutes of homework pretty consistently but didn't ever manage forty-five minutes at all when you moved right up to that longer stretch, backtrack to an intermediate stage like fifteen or twenty minutes. One excellent feature of shaping is that it's very forgiving. If you move forward too quickly and don't get the behavior you want, just backtrack to an intermediate step and move forward more gradually from there to where you want to go. Don't fall for the common parental myth about backtracking as giving in, being weak, or beginning a deadly slide down a slippery slope—misreadings of shaping that tie one hand behind your back as you try to effectively use the tools introduced in this chapter.

The second shaping error is a variant of the first one. Occasionally, parents provide incentives for outcomes rather than for progress along the way. A good example of this error comes from businesses such as fast-food restaurants that offer some special reward (money, food) for anyone who brings in a report card with all As. Such a long-delayed all-consequence "program" is guaranteed to fail. No kid who isn't already earning As will be induced to suddenly earn them by the promise of free super-size fries in the remote future. The approach of this book emphasizes reinforced practice and developing skills and habits. If those are solidly developed, outcomes are likely to be positive, but we rarely focus on some distant outcome. The process, rather than the outcome in isolation, builds the desired behaviors. One could make a similar argument about the increasingly widespread practice of pegging the pay of teachers to their students' test scores at the end of the term. This use of consequences encourages the teacher to get the outcome, no matter what. One way is to teach to the test with little regard for building students' study habits and intellectual range; another is to give students the answers to the tests, a kind of cheating we're likely to see more of as such policies become more common.

What should you take away from this brief survey of errors in developing behavior? Concentrate on providing reinforcement for processes (the specific desired behaviors) leading to outcomes (some longer-term goal, like a character trait). Provide reinforcers for studying, doing homework, and talking at the dinner table about something learned at school or read as homework. These will also be effective in improving outcomes, but providing reinforcement just for outcomes (getting mostly or all As) does not teach the requisite behaviors, doesn't develop habits, and can even encourage behaviors you are against, like cheating. I mention this in the context of shaping because going for outcomes over process—the end result without the steps to get there—amounts to a kind of negative opposite of shaping.

The most important concept

The key concept of this chapter and of this book is *practice of the desired behavior.* We want the behavior to occur so that consequences can be applied. Do the behavior, get the consequences; do the behavior, get the consequences. In the next chapter I refer to this as *reinforced practice,* to emphasize both the behavior occurring and the positive consequences that follow. A key part of practice is specifying the goal that one has in mind. Once you've identified it, you can work toward it with shaping, simulation, and/or jump-starting.

Conclusion

Behavior refers to what you want to change. The change may be an end in itself, like getting your child to do homework, or a path toward broad characteristics—like honesty or showing respect—that you wish your child to have. It is important to specify in concrete terms the behavior that you would like to change. More often than not, parents (and teachers, spouses—all of us) focus on the behavior we don't like and want to get rid of. The place to start is describing the positive opposite, that specific behavior you would like in place of the objectionable one. Sometimes the opposite is easy. I want my spouse to stop leaving the cap off the toothpaste! The positive opposite is, obviously, putting the cap on the toothpaste container. But for interpersonal behavior (stop teasing, stop shouting, stop picking on your angelic sister who can do no wrong), identifying the positive opposite requires a little more work. It's worthwhile to do it, though. We insist on this work because we can eliminate behaviors much more effectively when we focus on developing behaviors to replace them. Sometimes we just want to develop positive behavior when there's no negative one in its place to get rid of. Here, too, ask the same basic questions: What is the behavior you want? What would it look like? Answers to these questions greatly influence the effectiveness of the intervention.

When you draw on the important behavioral parts of the ABC approach, these reminders may help:

Dos

- Specify the positive behavior you want in concrete terms, even if your primary goal is to get rid of annoying or disturbing behavior.
- If there is a sequence or set of separate behaviors, specify each one and the order in which they occur; it will make the program much more effective.
- Use shaping to begin to develop the behavior you specified.
- Be patient with shaping (with both yourself and the child); we

are building habits, and moving slowly is usually the best way to do that so behavior takes the form you like and is locked in.
- If the behavior never occurs, set up simulations so you can use antecedents, shaping, and consequences to develop the behavior.
- If the child has the behavior well established but does not do it now, try jump-starting the behavior. Remember, "well established" means the child has done this behavior often in the past, not just that he "knows" (understands) what to do.
- Combine all the techniques in this chapter with antecedents as we discussed in the previous chapter—good antecedents (prompts, setting events) really speed up the process of developing behavior.
- Keep in mind the goal—we want the behavior to be practiced often, and ABCs are directed toward that intention.

Don'ts
- Don't identify general qualities like honesty or altruism as the starting point to change behavior. Start with specific behaviors and work toward them.
- Don't think that because a person knows how to do something that he or she will do it, will do it consistently, and will not need special help to develop the habit of doing it.
- Don't be frustrated because one child can do a behavior without a lot of effort on your part and another child requires shaping or other special techniques. There are enormous differences among all of us as people; this is the norm.

3

Reinforcing Good Behavior
C for Consequences

Consequences are what happen after a behavior: reward, punishment, or nothing at all. Each type of consequence can have a significant effect on whether a behavior continues or drops out—and that's true even when there's no consequence at all after the behavior, because even the lack of a consequence can influence behavior. I will take each type of consequence in turn over the course of two chapters. I'll start in this chapter with using rewards, the technical term for which is *positive reinforcement,* and then in the next chapter deal with punishment and also *extinction,* which is the technical name for purposeful ignoring of behavior.

First, let me say that consequences present a special challenge to us at the Yale Parenting Center because it's the section of the toolkit that parents who come to us for help typically have the most experience with. Antecedents might come as a new idea to them, and the notion of shaping and other such approaches to responding to a child's behavior might take some getting used to, but if they already have strong convictions about any aspect of parenting, it's likely to be in the area of consequences. After all, punishment is a consequence, and parents often have a lot of experience with punishment. But punishment is the least important and least effective kind of consequence.

The subject of consequences isn't as obvious as it might appear at first. The research offers us plenty of practical guidance and insight, some of which may well strike you as counterintuitive. At the center of this chapter is positive reinforcement, a powerful technique for building up the behaviors you want, and therefore for eliminating behaviors you don't want. You have a lot of options when you use positive reinforcement; I'll devote this chapter to putting them in your toolkit and showing you how to use them.

Your consequences toolkit

Positive reinforcement refers to the practice of using reinforcing consequences to increase the chances that a behavior will be repeated in the future. In this chapter I freely use the term *reinforcer* rather than *reinforcing consequences,* just to keep it simpler. I would just say "reward," but there's a subtle difference between a reinforcer and a reward. A *reward* is something that a person likes and regards as valuable. If you ask a child to list rewards, she'll probably list toys, special food treats, a pony, whatever age-appropriate goodies strike her as desirable. A *reinforcer* is something that is shown to increase behavior if employed systematically as a consequence following behavior. Often, rewards—money for an adult, say, or toys for children—are reinforcers. That is, the recipient views them as valuable, *and* they can change behavior. Yet there are many reinforcers that your child might not identify as particularly rewarding—for instance, your child might very well not describe your attention and praise as valued rewards—but nevertheless function as strong reinforcers. There's a lesson that makes this distinction important: even if your child does not identify something as a reward, it can still change behavior; and, in a complementary way, just because a person says something is rewarding does not automatically mean that it can be used as a reinforcer and effectively change behavior.

There are several types of reinforcers to be used in positive reinforcement. We focus on two that are most useful.

Praise and attention: Paying attention to a specific behavior and de-livering approval for it in the form of a positive statement, a smile, a touch. This is not as self-evident as it sounds. It often requires a conscious effort to get in the habit of paying positive attention to the behaviors you want, rather than the usual routine of reacting nega-tively to the behaviors you don't want.

Praise can be remarkably effective, but it has to be offered in a cer-tain way to change behavior. Simply saying "Good job!" a hundred times a day won't help much. I'll have more to say later in this chap-ter about how to use praise. But first, here's why I strongly advocate the use of praise to change behavior:

- When delivered properly, it can be very effective.
- It's similar to the attention and approval that people often use in everyday interactions, so using praise doesn't require parents to make the kind of changes in their habits that other (more artificial, less natural) reinforcers like a points system might entail. Turning to notice something a child did, smile and touch approvingly, or show disapproval with a look—all of these are "attention in the rough," habits that parents already have. We will craft that attention and approval to make a huge differ-ence in changing child behavior, but it's a refinement of what you already do.
- Unlike a system of points, you don't have to keep track of any-thing. We resort to points only if praise by itself is not working very well, if parents have trouble remembering to give praise, or if there are reasons to offer special incentives along with praise just to get the program going.
- Even if points are used, praise still is the reinforcer that gets the main emphasis.

Points, stars, stickers, and so on can be useful, as I've just men-tioned, if praise alone needs a boost at first. These are tokens that can be used to buy rewards. For example, a child can earn points for doing homework or going to bed on time. The points are like money and can be used to buy items or special activities—privileges like choosing the family's dinner menu, a slightly later bedtime, or extra time on the computer—that have prices based on the number of points.

Setting up a point chart has several steps, which include specifying

1. The target behaviors
2. The number of points that can be earned for performing the behaviors
3. The rewards (what the points can buy)
4. The number of points the rewards cost

The program can be simple. You can start it with only one or two behaviors you wish to develop, awarding one or two points for each behavior. Then have a reward list, a few items or privileges to buy that have low point values (two, three, four points) and then maybe something big—say, a twenty-five-point special treat or privilege—that the child can save up points to earn. These extra rewards are called "backup rewards," just to make it clear that your child will see getting the points, and of course your attention and praise, as a strong reinforcer in its own right.

Point chart is the term used most frequently in parenting programs. The technical name for a point chart is a *token economy,* emphasizing that the tokens (points, stars, and so on) are just the medium of exchange. Token economies have been used effectively with many different types of people and in many different situations, including the home, schools, hospitals, daycare centers, nursing homes, the military, colleges (for example, to reduce alcohol consumption, to improve practice performances on athletic teams), and business and industry (for example, to improve workers' safety practices and punctuality). In short, such programs have been very effective in many different contexts—and yet the points and charts are not absolutely necessary. That is, there's no inherent magic in a point chart; the behavior could be changed with just improved prompts and shaping and praise. The tokens merely provide a good way to structure and prompt parent behavior, especially the systematic use of consequences.

• • •

Using reinforcers to build up a desired behavior seems straightforward enough, but, as with our other procedures, the *how*—exactly how the reinforcer is administered—determines whether it will effectively change behavior.

Using positive reinforcement to reduce and eliminate unwanted behaviors

It's a rule of thumb that positive reinforcement is always related to increasing some behavior. But we have to reckon with the fact that much of what parents want to accomplish is to decrease or get rid of behavior—interrupting, playing with food, picking on a sibling, talking back, lying, stealing, . . . the list is endless. Can positive reinforcement help in getting rid of these behaviors? Yes. In fact, positive reinforcement is the *only* reliable way to eliminate these behaviors. So here I'll run through some reinforcement-based techniques for reducing or eliminating behaviors.

1. Reinforcement of positive opposites. In general, when you want to eliminate any behavior, whether it's a child's, spouse's, or colleague's, you begin with the very first step: Identify the positive opposite, the goal toward which you want to work. This means describing precisely what behaviors you do want to see in place of those you want to eliminate. Once you have that goal in view, you can use the ABCs—antecedents, behaviors, consequences—to reinforce the behavior you do want, always being careful not to accidentally attend to behavior you don't want. But it all flows from the first step: What is the behavior you want?

This first step is vitally important. At the Yale Parenting Center, at the end of our parent training, we present a set of common hypothetical situations in which we ask parents how they would get rid of some annoying behavior—rudeness at the dinner table, say, or acting up at the supermarket. We know we have been effective if in each case the parent begins by saying something like "Well, the positive opposite behavior we want would be . . ." When parents answer by skipping the first step and going straight to a consequence, like time out or ignoring the behavior, we know that we have been only mildly effective with them—that is, those strategies are OK, but they're not the first place to start and also not very effective as behavior-change procedures. You can't reinforce the positive opposite until you've identified it, and if you can't reinforce the positive opposite, it's very difficult to get rid of an unwanted behavior. You don't like the way your spouse squeezes the toothpaste from the middle of the tube? Go ahead, keep complaining about it, shake your head, endlessly repeat lines like "Why can't you just squeeze the @&%! toothpaste from the bottom of the tube? Is that too much to ask?" It will get you nowhere. But if after five or twenty-five years of this you switch to reinforcing positive opposites and using ABCs, you'll get somewhere. And the first step is identifying the behavior you want: in this case, squeezing the toothpaste tube from the bottom.

One father, Ray, conducted business from home, spending much of his workday dealing with suppliers whose goods he sold on his website. His "office" was actually in a corner of the dining room. He was on the phone often, and his business depended on it. His older child was six years old and at school most of the day; but his four-year-old daughter, Anna, developed the habit of talking to Daddy and asking for things when he was on the phone. She constantly interrupted him. "Can I go out to play? Is it OK to eat something now? When will you be off the phone? Can you play with me?" It was as if a phone call had become a cue for Anna to talk to her father. On the weekends, her brother joined her in interrupting Ray's calls.

Interrupting is a particularly interesting problem, from my point of view, because it's hard to ignore, and if it is ignored, the child will often just escalate until the interruption can no longer be ignored, at which point the adult either gives in to the request, shouts out a reprimand, or screams to his spouse to get in here and deal with the kids. The process is a good example of the power of attention to inappropriate behavior and the wrong kind of shaping, which in this case produced more and more intense interruptions. That's what was happening to Ray, the work-at-home dad. Business calls became occasions for a household upheaval, frequently culminating in a meltdown.

What to do? Well, you know where to begin: What exactly is the behavior you want? In this case, Ray wanted Anna to make no requests during a call and to make any request before or after the call. Now, put yourself in his place and think ABCs. Start with antecedents. What can you do before you get a call? When you're not on the phone, you can calmly tell the child to please not interrupt. You should explain exactly what counts as interrupting, and explain to her that your answer to anything she asks for during a call is automatically no, but if she waits until you're off the phone to ask, the answer could be yes or could be no, depending on the question, but you'll do your best to make it yes, if you can.

When a new behavior is developing, prompts right before the behavior are likely to be especially effective. But Ray couldn't know exactly when a call was about to come in, so he explained everything to his daughter as his workday began. When the first ring of a call came through and Anna was visibly nearby, he said to her, "OK, Anna, now's your chance to see if you can wait to talk until the phone call is done." (This was a nice, quick little challenge.)

We thought Ray could use shaping effectively in this situation, too—that a partial sample of a behavior should be praised as well. We decided that two minutes into the first couple of calls during a given day, Ray would put his hand over the receiver of the phone and go over to Anna and smile, give a big OK hand gesture with his arm outstretched above his head, quietly whisper praise for not interrupting, and give her a gentle touch if he could. A couple of these per day would be great. We wanted the praise for not interrupting at all to be immediate and really effusive. If Anna was interrupting every single call, giving Ray no chance to reinforce not-interrupting, it would be time to do some simulations to practice not-interrupting—he could call it the Phone Game and make sure she got plenty of praise, points, whatever it took, as a result of doing the right thing while he pretended to be on the phone.

Now, the consequences. We wanted Ray to reinforce the positive opposite, which was Anna making requests before or after the call, and that he would not attend to, turn around to face, or make eye contact with her if she made a request during the call. Requests made when Ray was not on the phone should be praised. "This is great! You're asking me for a snack when I'm not on the phone!" We reminded Ray to add a pat or a hug, and between calls to praise either no interrupting or less interrupting.

Ray and his wife really liked the idea for the program because it was concrete. Sometimes the mother would be nearby in the house and could praise Anna (or, on weekends, both children) for playing nicely and not talking to her father when he was on the phone.

Ray made or received at least twenty calls a day. We asked him to tally each call and put a check mark next to it if he was interrupted. Interruptions went down from about thirteen each day to five in the first two days of the program, and then to zero after five days. We needed two weekends to get rid of weekend call interruptions by the six-year-old—not very much practice could occur for the older child during the week. Eight days into the program, the mom and dad stopped the praise during the week. Interruptions were holding steady at zero, and they praised that, but it seemed that the need for a carefully executed praise program was over. After two weekends, interruptions seemed like a nonissue. Four and then eight weeks later, Ray reported one interruption, but he had ignored it, and interrupting stopped being an issue in that home.

This was a very typical household situation. Your child teases the pet, does not pick up his laundry, comes into your bedroom too early on a Sunday morning, spills food on the floor . . . just keep filling in the rest. Your first step, in response, should be to ask, "What's the positive opposite?"

Reinforcing positive opposites is your all-in-one tool, useful in almost all situations. But there are two more specialized variations of using reinforcement to reduce behaviors that you'll find useful to have in your kit.

2. *Reinforcing other behavior that isn't quite the positive opposite.* What if the child never seems to do *any* of the positive opposite be-

havior? Sometimes a child does something frequently that you want to get rid of. Positive opposites are easy to identify, and of course you do that. But if he never does anything like the positive opposite, how can you reinforce it? One option is to use simulations to practice the desired behavior—a B (of the ABCs) option we discussed in the previous chapter. Also, shaping was a B strategy we discussed in that chapter, but here it seems as if the child is not even close to showing crumbs of the desired behavior that we could build on to develop the final behaviors we want. So you need another way to address the problem, and there's a C (consequence) solution that you can turn to.

This solution consists of reinforcing everything or virtually everything the child does *other than* the undesired behavior. Essentially, we look at the child and say, for the moment, we are going to classify everything he does as either (1) what we want to eliminate or (2) everything else. Everything else is the "other" behavior. We adopt this when the behaviors we want to eliminate are so frequent that we need to get some control right away.

I had a memorable introduction to this approach when I worked with a ten-year-old child named Evan in a regular fifth-grade elementary school classroom. The teacher asked for my help because one of her students—Evan—was distressingly active. *Active* is really a pale word to describe this child. Evan walked on the desks during lessons, stepping from desk to desk, stomping on other students' work as he went. While he did this he talked out loud, saying things to the teacher as if nothing else was going on. She said he was never in his seat. I observed the class for a few periods on separate days and the teacher wasn't exaggerating: this child just never sat down.

What to reinforce? A positive opposite would be sitting quietly in his seat, doing the work, and paying attention. But this package of behavior never occurred, and in fact none of its components ever occurred, which meant that shaping did not seem possible, at least at first. So we decided to begin with praising Evan for any behavior other than walking on desks or talking out loud. Sometimes he was silent for a little while. True, he'd be standing next to his desk, and he wouldn't be working, but during these moments he wasn't doing either of the two behaviors the teacher wanted to reduce: walking across the desks and talking out loud. It wasn't quite the ideal positive opposite of his disruptive behavior, but it was better, so it was a place to start.

I stayed in the room for thirty minutes for two days to help prompt the teacher. I had a sheet of colored paper (two sheets stapled together, actually), one side red and the other side green. When Evan was engaging in anything other than the behaviors we wanted to eliminate, I immediately held up the green sheet. This was a prompt to the teacher to praise him and, if feasible (depending on where she was standing), to do this up close, quietly, and with a physical pat. If it wasn't feasible for her to get over to him, she just praised out loud from where she was. It was important to help the teacher because the usual thing we do, the instinctive thing for a species wired by evolution to overreact to negative stimulus, is to let things go unremarked upon when behavior is fine and therefore not threatening.

The teacher quickly mastered this approach, and in the thirty minutes I was there she went over to Evan three times—I prompted the first two; she did the third on her own. (I was fading my prompts to her, a technique you learned in chapter one.) On the second day, I went to class and she went over to him twice unprompted. She did not see her third opportunity to reinforce Evan's better-than-awful behavior, as she was turned facing the board, so I held up the green side of the sheet as soon as she turned around, and she reinforced the behavior then. We had agreed that we would do this program only in the morning, to see if we were having any effect, and then if it went well, we would extend it to the afternoon. The main reason for this was that administering reinforcement (praise) correctly and frequently is hard work, and she had other students to attend to.

After a few days, it was clear that this regimen greatly increased not walking on desks and not talking out loud. Now, occasionally, Evan was even sitting in his seat, a behavior that previously had never seemed to occur. Now we switched from praising any nondisruptive behavior to focusing on sitting in his seat, a component of the positive opposite we hoped to develop. Any time Evan was in his seat, even if he wasn't paying attention or doing his work, the teacher praised that behavior specifically. If he was also focusing on a classroom task, she added special praise for that. This was slow going (after all, the teacher did have a room full of other students to teach) and it took a few weeks, but we were able to get Evan to a point where he spent most of his time in his seat, and we completely eliminated walking on the desks, his most wildly disruptive behavior. As a bonus, his habit of talking out of turn in class dropped out on its own. Apparently, his talking was linked to walking on the desks, and when we eliminated desk walking the talking went with it.

The excellent effects of this approach, reinforcing other behavior short of the positive opposite, have been evident in many cases in which we've worked with parents in the home. For example, two brothers, four and five years old, were constantly arguing, teasing, and picking on each other. The parents found this surprising and annoying—surprising because they had expected that their sons would appreciate having a natural playmate in the household, and annoying because there was no letup in the conflict. The only times of peace came when one of the boys was not home (the five-year-old was in school). I first queried the parents on what exactly they wanted to see, the positive opposites. They wanted parallel play (in the same room without fighting) or cooperative play (both doing the same thing together, like playing with blocks or even just watching TV together) or peace during some activity other than play (for example, dinner, drives to church in the car, errands). The parents explained to me that there was no significant stretch of peace when the boys were together, and they asked if there was any way to get control of the constant teasing. From among our B (for behavior) options we could have chosen simulations, a Getting-Along game they could play. But we could also take the C (consequences) route and address the problem with reinforcement of other behavior.

We defined "other behavior" to mean any time the boys were in view of each other (in the same room, in the car) and there was a brief period without their annoying each other or bickering. The program had two parts. When the boys were together and not bickering, one of the parents would praise them. The boys were also told that if they could be together for two minutes without arguing, they would receive a point. So we weren't really reinforcing a positive opposite. Instead, we reinforced anything other than bickering, teasing, and being annoying. Another way to say "anything but" is "other behavior," and that's why this approach is called reinforcing other behavior.

The points were earned as a team. The boys earned or didn't earn the points together—so there was never a situation in which just one boy could earn points. And the rewards they could buy with the points went to both boys, never just one. So, for example, they could spend four points on staying up fifteen minutes longer before bedtime; both boys got to stay up. When they accumulated four points, they could cash them in for that reward, or they could agree to let the points "ride" for some other reward. The parents, who knew their sons well, asked what would happen if the boys argued over the reward and couldn't agree on one. We explained that the boys had to agree on the reward, and they had to get the same one. If they bickered and couldn't agree on one, no reward was given that night, but they could bank the points until the next day. (It's important that you choose rewards that your child really values, not just things you think he should value.) This worked out pretty well. Both boys placed high value on extending their bedtime and on playing certain backyard games that required their father's participation, so it wasn't hard to get them to agree on spending their points.

When they praised, the parents exclaimed over how big and grown-up the brothers were acting. They were sure to be effusive, and to be specific about what the boys were doing: "You're sitting together with no arguing." And they remembered to add a physical pat or touch when they could. After about three days of this, the boys were still bickering, but there were stretches of not-bickering and even moments when they actually spoke nicely to each other. The parents stepped up their praise at such moments and gave special bonus points (five). Over time the parents made a gradual move from reinforcing other behavior (anything but . . .) to reinforcing some of the positive opposites—like the boys speaking nicely to each other—they had identified at the beginning. In a week, the parents felt there were great changes and kept up the praise but stopped the point program. (They let the brothers trade in all leftover points for a major weekend outing.) The bickering did not stop completely, but it fell to a manageable level, and the parents felt that some amount of bickering was to be expected. They felt the program was successful, especially because the boys actually started to play more together, rather than merely tolerating each other's existence.

This was another case in which we started out with reinforcing any behavior other than the disruptive behavior, and then, as we began to see some of the positive opposites occur, we moved more specifically to reinforcing those.

3. *Reinforcing disruptive behaviors when they happen less often.* This one seems really counterintuitive, but stay with me. Let's say a behavior—shouting, swearing, saying something nasty, being aggressive—occurs ten times a day, or ten times before lunch. One way to eliminate the behavior is to shape fewer and fewer instances of the behavior. The child can be praised if he engages in the behavior only eight times. This seems distressingly wrong to many parents, and I often hear some version of "Let me get this straight: my child is saying nasty things and I'm praising him for it?" Yes, that's what's happening, and you're doing it because you're shaping the process of fewer and fewer of these nasty things being said until you can eliminate them entirely.

For example, I worked with a seven-year-old boy, Ted, who bullied other children in his classroom. Once I heard about this, of course, I asked the teacher to specify what she meant and what bullying meant for this boy. He teased others, pushed them, and messed up their work as they tried to write at their desks. Along with that, he said nasty things about them—how stupid they were, how funny they looked, and so on. As soon as the class settled in at the beginning of the school day, he started to pick on children seated near him, and he kept it up all day.

We wanted to reinforce the positive opposite, interacting with others nicely, but Ted seemed to have only two modes: bullying or silence. We told Ted he could earn a very special treat for himself and the entire class. If he could do what was asked, the class would get an extra recess or a special mystery story right before lunch break. Each day that Ted earned the privilege, he could choose which one it would be, recess or the story. To earn it, he had to not pick on other people for fifteen minutes after class started, at 8:30 a.m. (We of course specified exactly what picking on people consisted of.) If he did not bully anyone by 8:45, he would earn the reward. We told him this was hard to do and we were not sure he could do it (all great antecedents here; see chapter one), but we would give it a try.

With all of that buildup, on the first day Ted met the criterion and the teacher quietly went to him at 8:45 and told him, effusively, that because he hadn't said anything nasty to anyone, the class would earn a reward, no matter what he did for the rest of the morning. And now he could choose the reward! Ted was pretty mild for the rest of the morning; he engaged in a little bullying, but for him it was good. (We asked the teacher to protect any victims from being upset, intimidated, or hurt as soon as she saw any sign of bullying, by asking the victim to come over to her. We wanted her to try very temporarily to not attend to Ted—the risk was too great that she would accidentally reinforce bullying that way.) We continued this for three more days. One day he didn't earn the privilege, but after two days in a row on which he did, we said, "OK, now it gets really hard"—a good challenge antecedent. "Can you go for a whole half-hour?"

And so on. Over three and a half weeks we shaped the behavior so that he received the special reward at the end of the day, rather than before lunch, and if he made it through the whole day, there was an extended recess *and* a story. Then we praised him for making it for two and then three days in a row. His bullying and nasty comments were mostly eliminated. Added to this all along was reinforcing of any positive prosocial interaction—we tried to catch him when he engaged in positive opposite behavior once in a while. That part made the program much more likely to be effective. Ted didn't in fact have only two modes, bullying and silence. Like a lot of bullies, he actually did have some interactions with other children that were fine—chatting in line, talking about a TV show or something odd that had happened in a game, that kind of thing. We viewed these regular, neutral exchanges as prosocial and praised them whenever they occurred. We "caught him being socially functional," in other words, and reinforced it.

So in addition to systematically eliminating Ted's bullying, the undesired behavior, by shaping longer and longer periods without the behavior occurring, we also reinforced its positive opposite—prosocial interactions with other children. We needed to do both because merely increasing the non-bullying interactions might not have eliminated the bullying; there was enough time in the day for Ted to bully a little and get along a little. So we worked on decreasing the bullying *and* building up its positive opposite.

This example focuses on gradually decreasing the frequency of a behavior. One can also take a behavior that has many components—I previously mentioned a tantrum that might include hitting, swearing, shouting, and crying for a long time. Less intense versions can be shaped by concentrating on knocking out one of the components at a time, or reducing its intensity, until there's not much tantrum left, and then none at all. That means that for a short period you'll be praising "good" tantrums, which I hope no longer feels utterly insane to you.

How to use reinforcers so they actually work

Positive reinforcement puts some extremely useful new tools in your toolkit. But, as we saw in previous chapters, outlining your options in using positive reinforcement is just part of the information you need to use this approach effectively. It's the *what,* and now I need to talk about the *how.* Reinforcers have to be provided in a special way, and that applies to whether praise or tokens or other rewards are used. If they aren't provided this way, they don't work very well. So, the *how:*

1. Provide the reinforcer (praise, for instance) immediately after the behavior whenever you can. Behavior and reinforcer need to be closely connected in time. If, one or two minutes after your child cleaned up her room, you say, "You picked up all the clothes in your room and you made your bed, too; that's really great," your praise can make that same behavior much more likely in the future. If you say the same thing to her one

day after she cleans up her room, it's not likely to change that behavior at all.

2. Convey exactly what the reinforcer is given for. What exactly are those behaviors you want to increase in the future? Specifying exactly what they are will really help. So "You picked up all the clothes in your room and you made your bed, too; that's really great" is much more effective than "Good job!" Of course, it's OK to say "Good job" (enthusiastically), if it's followed by statements of exactly what the job was and what made it good.

3. Use a high-quality reinforcer. This doesn't mean expensive rewards. It means, for instance, that when praising young children you need to be effusive and enthusiastic. Mediocre, nonchalant, and low-key praise for young children just does not work as well. Quality is also influenced by combining verbal praise with a touch or positive physical gesture—rubbing the child's shoulder, a high-five, a hug—whatever suits the parent-child style. The idea is to do something physical, approving, and affectionate. If points are being used, do not give one point for the behavior if the child needs at least twenty points to buy a reward. There's no advantage in being stingy. Make it worthwhile and relatively easy for your child to get enough points to buy the cheapest (in points) reward. Remember, you will drop all of the points soon enough, so this is just temporary. Also, when points are given, pair that with effusive praise, and be as enthusiastic as the market will bear: that is, with young children, extremely enthusiastic (think of a game-show host communicating hearty approval to a colleague on a neighboring mountaintop); with older children, less effusive; with teenagers, low-key but still clearly pleased.

4. As a behavior is developing, try to provide the reinforcer every time the behavior occurs. This is not always practical, but try. Performing the behavior will occur at a higher rate and the habit can be developed sooner if you can provide

the reward every time, or close to it, that the behavior is performed.

These requirements might seem at first blush as if they're not very special, but bear in mind that most programs for changing children's behavior fail because the reinforcer is delayed too long after the behavior or is given irregularly (not even close to almost every time), and/or the quality of reinforcers is really poor. For example, parents who come to the Yale Parenting Center routinely tell us that they already do praise their child often and well. Then we work individually with these parents to train them to maximize the effectiveness of praise, and they can see that praise to change behavior effectively is very different from the usual praise most parents give. It's a lesson that I, too, had to learn as a parent. Knowing what the research says and actually doing it are two different things.

Similarly, it's hard to find a parent in the developed world who has not used a point chart—and chances are that point chart has failed to help in any way. The key to success lies in the delivery, in the *how*.

One very common reason for the failure of a point program is that a parent is misled to see magic in the points themselves, not in the key principles of positive reinforcement that the points are designed to facilitate. Also, as we have noted, points are consequences—and consequences are just part of the ABCs that are needed for effective and long-lasting behavior change. When points are used, sometimes they distract parents from praising, but praise, the constant in any reward program, will be the main basis for changing behavior. Points are almost never a substitute or replacement for praise. Just the opposite, in fact: most of the time, praise alone will do the job and points aren't needed.

One mom who came to see me at the Yale Parenting Center wanted her eight-year-old daughter, Isabella, nicknamed Izzie, to practice the piano every day. She had gone through the usual parenting ploys that we have all used: complaining that lessons were expensive and would be a complete waste if Izzie did not practice, declaring that she was embarrassed and ashamed because the teacher said that Izzie clearly was not trying very hard, threatening to withhold TV and computer time if Izzie didn't practice, and so on. That's all standard parenting. The effects of the mom's ploys were predictable; they didn't help, and now the nightly drama of practicing the piano had become a parent-versus-child battleground.

The mom went on the Web for help and found point charts as an option. She thought that giving Izzie points on a chart for practicing would do the trick. The mom printed out a sheet to keep track of points and announced to Izzie that the old regime of taking away TV and computer time was over. Izzie could watch and indulge. If she practiced thirty to forty minutes of piano, as her teacher asked, she would get ten points each time. Any week when she earned forty or more points, they would do a special activity on the weekend—a movie of Izzie's choice, shopping for one small toy, going to a nearby amusement park.

This program had some benefits. For one thing, losing TV and computer time as punishment definitely would not have worked or made Izzie like or want to play the piano, so dumping that was a step in the right direction.

But the program didn't work. Or, rather, it worked on the first night, probably because the novelty of it all and Mom's enthusiasm for a new approach piqued Izzie's interest. But she rapidly lost interest in it, and now the nagging went like this: "Why aren't you practicing? Look at all the good things we can do if you practice."

The mother came to us for help, enormously frustrated and perplexed as to why the program she started had not worked. We explained to her that the program failed because:

- There was no shaping. Don't start by requiring the full thirty or forty minutes of practice time to qualify for points—that alone would make the program ineffective. We start where the child is—if practice is zero minutes, we begin with three to five minutes. As this becomes consistent, we can move to more.
- What exactly constituted "practice" wasn't specified very well. Izzie should know exactly what was expected of her. Just sitting on the bench plinking keys? Doing specific tasks that the music teacher prescribed?

- The reinforcer was very delayed—until the end of the week—and that alone would doom the program to failure. Early in developing behavior there should be no or minimal delay between the desired behavior and the consequence. As behavior develops, delays in the consequences are fine, but early delays mean early program failure.
- Praise was not a part of this program. That, too, all by itself, could readily explain why the program didn't work. Think of points as an addition to a praise program rather than the other way around. Basically, your praise and attention to your child are hugely influential, and a couple of trinkets or privileges are not anywhere near as effective. Also, using praise could help bridge the delay of the reinforcer until the weekend activity.
- The mom didn't take advantage of several kinds of A (antecedents) and B (behaviors) options that would have improved her chances of success. For instance, at the beginning, sitting with her child, taking turns, doing a simulated Practice the Piano game for a few minutes to get more points; having the child teach the mom one of her exercises; listening to piano versions of songs Izzie liked, to give her an extra incentive to learn to play the instrument; going to a music store to pick out the music for some songs Izzie liked and could play would be great. Alternatively, the mom could be in the room with Izzie for the first few minutes and then out of the room for a few more minutes (coming back in to praise when those minutes went well), and gradually remove herself from the scene of practice. We want children to like playing their instruments, and the parent can do a lot to help that happen, especially by using antecedents effectively—in this case, the mom could use her presence to help or join in, then gradually fade that presence.
- Points can be a distraction (to the parent) if the parent believes that the points themselves will improve behavior. The action is not where the points are; it's in repeated practice and use of As, Bs, and Cs to make that happen. And remember that when it

comes to the Cs, we lead with our strength—parent praise delivered with the ingredients I've stressed: be effusive, state the exact behaviors being praised, add something nonverbal like an affectionate touch.

That seems like a lot of stuff to fix, but actually all Izzie's mother had to do was to make a few changes for the program to be effective.

First, we started with ten minutes of her sitting with Izzie as a way to begin practice—this was an antecedent: "Let's start *our* practice now"—and then walking to the room with the mom's arm around Izzie or holding her hand. (Use of "our" is a good setting event because it begins with sharing the task, working together, and not someone ordering someone else to do something.) The mom asked Izzie to start with one exercise the teacher had given her and to explain it to the mom to help her understand. Putting the child in this teaching position gave her more control over the situation. (Being in control has effects similar to those of choice—it increases the likelihood of engaging in the desired behaviors.) Izzie wasn't always being told what to do but could tell her mother how to do it. Then they played something from the lesson for that week for the rest of the ten minutes. When the ten minutes ended (the mom set up a kitchen timer in the room where Izzie practiced), they got up and stopped, or they could work on "Chopsticks" or some other simple piece just for fun; Izzie could choose. More often than not, she chose to do it. Among other things, she enjoyed being better at "Chopsticks" than her mother was.

After several days of this, the mother walked her daughter to the room and had her start without her: "You get started; I'll be back in a minute." The mother returned in a minute or two. Practice continued. We increased the amount of time in five- to ten-minute increments and trimmed the amount of time the mom was in the room. Soon she was coming in ten minutes and then twenty minutes after Izzie had begun, and finally only at the end of the practice to play "Chopsticks" or a Christmas carol they both liked and had added to their repertoire of duet practice. Many of these practice sessions ended in laughter as they practiced the fun piece and made little improvisations, as when Izzie introduced part of "Chopsticks" in the middle of a Christmas carol. The tone of the practice and parent-child exchanges about it had changed.

The mother praised Izzie at first for going to practice sessions with her, for starting on an exercise, for teaching her about her lesson so nicely, then for practicing while the mom was not even in the room, and eventually for doing the whole practice. I suggested she contact the teacher about the program and make sure the teacher noticed and commented on any improvements evident in the lessons themselves. That was a delayed reinforcer for more and better practice, since Izzie saw the teacher only once a week, but it helped.

We eventually ended with the mom providing intermittent praise for practice. Also, we wanted to give the child some options about practice. One day a week she could take a break from practicing if she wanted to. Izzie selected this option the first week and then irregularly in the following months. Also, during the week she began to show a behavior that made her mother very happy: Izzie would occasionally sit at the piano outside of her practice sessions and play an exercise or song from the lesson.

By fixing the program, it might seem at first as if we made it harder for the mom to get Izzie to practice. After all, there was more parent involvement in the early stage, and the mom had to do more prompting and then fade her presence. But really we just gave her a little more focus, a little more purpose. Effective programs are not more complex than ineffective ones. The difference usually lies in tinkering with the *how,* and in fact ineffective programs usually require more work because they don't produce progress, everyone is stressed, and after two days, two weeks, or two months everyone is still at square one because the program didn't work.

Perhaps the best example of constructive tinkering in this program was in the use of praise—hardly a rearrangement of anyone's life or routine. Usual parental praise ("That's good, Tommy") is not nearly as effective as the praise we have been talking about. So a critical part of Izzie's piano practice program was having the mother praise in a way that would be much more effective—that is, enthusiastically specifying exactly what the behaviors were that were being praised, and with some physical gesture. Learning to praise that way takes a little work at first, but in the long run praising effectively, in ways that produce results that allow you to fade and then discontinue such praise for a desired behavior, is far less work than saying "Good job!" ten thousand times with no effect.

Putting it all together

You want your four-year-old boy to come over to you when you ask. He loves to run around, which is great, but he also likes to run away from you when you are at the park or walking to the park. He thinks it's loads of fun, but you are worried about his safety; you've even thought about one of those leashes for children. But you want to try a praise program first. The positive opposite is easily defined: coming to you when you ask, the first time. This never seems to occur, so—as we discussed in the last chapter—you set up a game to simulate walking to the park. You call this the Come-to-Me game. In the house you position yourself in different places—different corners of the living room, then in different rooms—and ask him to come to you. When he comes to you, you give him high-quality praise. That means you do it right away, and you do it every time he comes to you when you ask him to. Very effusively, you say, "That was GREAT! I asked you to come and you came right away!" and you lean over and give him a hug (the nonverbal component that, when added to your words, makes the reinforcer more effective). And you want to do this at least a couple of times a day for a week or so as your schedule allows. The key is to create repeated opportunities for your child to do the behavior and receive the reinforcers.

That sequence of reinforced practice—do the behavior, get the positive reinforcer, do it again—is the single most important idea in this book. There is no magic in the reinforcer all by itself, even if it's a ridiculously extravagant reward. Giving your child a pony as a reward won't help him get in the habit of coming to you when you ask him to. Only reinforced practice will get him there, even if the reinforcer is "nothing more" than your attention and praise. We use antecedents to get the behavior to occur, and we use consequences to help lock it in. But the key is the middle part—repetition of the behavior—and providing effective reinforcers greatly increases the likelihood that the behavior will continue in the future.

Another example: Let's say you're shaping your preteen to clean her room. You have forgotten whether there is a throw rug, wall-to-wall carpet, or a hardwood floor under the months-old layers of discarded food packaging, dirty and "clean" clothes, books and loose pages, shoeboxes, and plastic bags from a variety of stores. You are shaping having clean sections of the room. You start off with having her clear one three-square-foot corner (she gets to choose which corner—good use of choice here) so that the floor is perfectly visible. She can't just pile the stuff up on another part of the floor; she has to show you that she put the stuff away. She says she's done for that morning and wants you to check. She earns points for doing this correctly and of course you also use praise. You go in and see that the space is clear, she shows you where the clothes are hung up in her closet, and there's a plastic bag of trash in the doorway ready to go downstairs. You praise with just a slightly raised voice. Teens often do not respond as well to really effusive praise, which they regard as embarrassingly uncool.

Science isn't ready to grapple with uncoolness as a research topic, but I can offer a thumbnail explanation for why you need to tone down your praise with a teenager. There's a brief period in life, spanning preadolescence and early adolescence, in which it may appear that parents, their values, and their approval move from being very positive in a child's eyes to being neutral or even negative. Two reassuring points are in order here. First, this does not happen with all or even most adolescents. Second, this is not their real view; they have not abandoned all your values, they still value you and need your input, and they do not in fact want to be alienated from them while they are on a biological, psychological, and social roller coaster set in motion by massive hormonal and brain changes and corresponding emotional and cognitive changes—a complex of upheaval that also, of course, contributes to changes in behavior. That said, you may find that your approval becomes embarrassing or irritating to your adolescent child, especially when your approval takes the form of a loud public reminder that your child is in fact a child and under your control. With an adolescent, effusiveness and public displays may be received as attacks on the child's developing sense of dignity. This means that the effusive, excited, and wonderful praise that worked so well when your child was younger has to change. Now more reserved, more private, and less intrusive praise is more effective. It will still work very well—if it's specific, immediate, paired with a physical gesture . . . you know the drill—but it needs to scale down. If you're wondering, as many parents do, how you can tell when to tone down the praise, the guidelines are easy on this. If there are consistent signs that your praise is aversive—your child grimaces, shies away from you, tries to cut you off, shows the clearest look of disgust you have ever seen, and so on—take those signs as a cue to tone down effusiveness. But don't make the mistake of taking such reactions as cues to stop praise. Instead, move to a quieter, more intimate style of praise—to low-key comments of approval delivered up close and in a low voice, paired with a light touch on the shoulder or a mimed high-five from across the room.

In the case of the preteen with the messy room who has taken the first steps toward cleaning it up, you still tell her that she did well, being sure to specify what she did, and then you give her a high-five or thumbs-up—still curbing your uncoolness, of course. Then you say, "OK, you earned five points on the chart, and you can cash those in for more computer time or credit on your iTunes account."

So the program proceeds. When the designated corner is clear on most days (let's say four out of five), the program extends to another corner. Now, to earn the points both corners have to be cleared, and of course two corners equals more points. You praise if only one corner of the room has been cleared, but you give points (plus praise, of course) if both are cleared. You might say something like "This is great; you kept that corner clear. I can't give you points because this other corner is not so clear, but we'll have another chance at points tomorrow." When faced with half-good or otherwise partially successful results, try to resist the urge to "caboose," the unhelpful habit of tacking a criticism onto your praise (as in "This corner's clean but this one's a pigsty"). Caboosing negates the good effects of the praise it follows. Just praise what was good, and remind the child what she can do to get even more reinforcers, like points.

One family working with the Yale Parenting Center on such a clean-room program eventually got to the point of having all of the room clear except one corner. The daughter then asked her parents if she could leave that one corner without having to worry about keeping it perfectly clean. The parents asked us about that and we said this was a very reasonable request, it gave the child control over her own room, and saying yes would show the child that her parents could compromise—all excellent things to do in parenting. We asked the parents to work out the specific boundaries of the messy corner in the room—"one corner" meant an area bounded by the end of the bed on one side and the beginning of the rug on the other, and so on. Also, the parents insisted that food was off limits even in the messy corner because it could lead to unacceptable problems like bad smells, insects, or rodents.

In shaping, as this program reflects (one corner, then add the next, and then the next), perfection is never required. Not every day and not every corner had to be perfect. The cliché "Perfect is the enemy of the good" applies here. We can build strong habits, consistency, and enduring characteristics, none of which requires demanding perfection. One can get excellent behavior by shaping, but perfection is usually unfair to demand of humans. The natural worry is "If I don't demand perfection now, won't my daughter just learn to be mediocre in everything?" No, she will find many things in life that compel her heart and enthusiasm, and your demanding that she do little tasks around the house with perfection is not likely to influence that.

Conclusion

"Consequences" refers to what follows behavior. This chapter focused on what should be the main type of consequences: positive reinforcement. This is a central component of virtually all behavior-change programs we are discussing because positive reinforcement is used to directly increase behaviors you wish to develop—and therefore, indirectly, to decrease and eliminate the behaviors you don't want. And when you reach into your toolkit for a consequence, be sure to grab praise first. This is the tool that will carry you very far as a reinforcer—if it's done right and contains the three critical ingredients: age-appropriate enthusiasm, a specific description of what you're praising, and a component of touch to go along with your words. With those ingredients, you can lock in the behaviors, habits, and broader characteristics you wish.

At the center of everything we're trying to accomplish is the concept of reinforced practice: we want the behavior to occur repeatedly (the practice part) and use consequences (reinforcement) to make that happen. This is important to mention because there is no magic in reinforcement (consequences) or in the antecedents either. Each is a critical means toward the end. We want the behavior to occur repeatedly so we can shape it, build consistency in the behavior (lock it in as a habit), and move on (fade and then stop the program as the behavior becomes a habit).

Positive reinforcement is all about building up the behaviors you want, but I realize that many of parents' most urgent goals have to do with decreasing and eliminating undesired behaviors. That's why I emphasize reinforcement of positive opposites. The importance of this will be even clearer in the next chapter when we get to punishment, the most used but often the least effective way of changing behavior.

When you use positive reinforcement, here are some things to keep in mind:

Dos

- Specify the behavior you want to develop in clear terms so you will be consistent in providing reinforcing consequences.
- Have a plan—what you want that behavior to look like when this program is over. Now identify steps along the way (shaping) that you will reinforce (for example, with praise). Without a plan, reinforcement is likely to be given unsystematically and will not change the child's behavior.

- Emphasize praise. Usually it works all by itself as the main consequence. If you include a point program, points are in addition to praise, not a replacement for it. For children age ten or eleven and under (but this is approximate), make sure your praise is effusive and followed by a very clear statement about exactly what behaviors you are praising, and then add something physical that is approving or affectionate (touch, pat, hug). For preteens and above (eleven to sixteen, depending on your judgment of the maturity of the child), the three ingredients (praise, statement, physical gesture) may need to change to accommodate the normal (but fortunately temporary) adolescent feeling that anything parents do, think, believe, or support is misguided and uncool. Praise quietly and not in a public way, but still do say exactly what you liked (no change on this) and add some physical gesture that is acceptable — it could be a high-five that just touches the child's hand, or a high-five in the air; it could be thumbs-up as a gesture indicating approval — something like that. If physical contact would be pushing it, a gesture will do.
- Deliver any reinforcer in the way that is required to change behavior, which means:
- Deliver it immediately after the behavior (rather than delaying it).
- Say exactly what you are praising — specify the behaviors.
- For young children, make that praise effusive — it makes a difference.
- Add nonverbal praise — touch, hug, affectionate pat on the shoulder, and so on.
- Try to reinforce often as the behavior is developing — every time or almost every time it occurs, as feasible.

Don'ts

- Don't improvise rewards or incentives for random behaviors that you want done around the house. Winging it will guarantee failure. Consequences are part of a systematic plan to develop particular behaviors or a set of behaviors. Repeated prac-

tice of a particular behavior or set of behaviors is the goal, and
using reinforcers to get that target behavior to occur repeatedly
is your aim.

- Don't confuse your ordinary nurturing and caring parenting
  with what we are focusing on in this book. Praise and hugs, for
  example, can be given in many ways and often. I am not saying that all praise, hugs, and touches should focus on changing
  behavior. If you are an affectionate parent, keep it up. If you
  are warm and loving with your child, do not change or stop. I
  am saying that when you have as a goal to increase or decrease
  a particular behavior, to develop habits, and to develop broad
  characteristics (honesty, consideration, respect), praise can
  now *also* be used strategically. When used in this strategic way,
  praise and hugs (consequences) have to be used systematically
  and in concert with other factors (antecedents, behaviors) to
  reach a goal.

- Don't make the mistake of thinking you need wildly attractive
  incentives to get the behavior you want. There's not much dem-
  onstrated correlation between the cost of rewards and their
  effectiveness as reinforcers. A trip to Disney World may be a
  whopper of a reward, but it could well turn out to be an ineffective reinforcer, while the privilege of picking what the family
  eats for dinner tonight may be an extremely effective reinforcer
  if it's properly used. And the whole notion of rewards, large or
  small, is secondary to the main point here. The crucial thing
  to bear in mind is that in the vast majority of instances, your
  attention and praise, used carefully in the ways I've suggested
  in this chapter, will be enough to develop the behaviors you
  desire.

4

Decreasing Misbehavior

More on Consequences

I devoted the entire previous chapter to positive reinforcement because it's the most effective way to use consequences to develop behavior. As I've explained, the key concept is reinforced practice—that is, getting the behavior to occur (the "practice" part) and following that with reinforcing consequences (the "reinforced" part) so the behavior will occur again. Arranging for many repetitions of this sequence allows for shaping and then developing the habit consistently.

But positive reinforcement is not the only kind of consequence. Reinforcers aren't the only response you can make to your child's behavior that influences whether it occurs again. Punishment is also a consequence, and it's part of everyday life, familiar to any parent—or, in fact, to any child or anyone who used to be a child. The same is true of another kind of consequence: not responding at all to a behavior, the technical term for which is *extinction*. There are, however, many nuances in how these kinds of consequences can be used to influence behavior, and each has more and less effective variations.

It's common for parents and other adults who have responsibility for children to rely heavily on punishment as a primary tool for changing behavior, but the best research says in no uncertain terms that if punishment has a useful role, it's as a secondary adjunct to positive reinforcement. If punishment worked best, I'd say so and urge you to rely on it, but it doesn't work best. Still, like not responding to behavior, punishment can indeed help change behavior, and I'll show you how to use both tools most effectively.

I'll consider punishment and not responding to behavior separately in this chapter, since each has its own unique qualities and effects. But they have one major trait in common. Both can change behavior, but not on their own. Whether they work depends completely on combining them with a program of positive reinforcement that develops behavior to replace the behavior you're trying to get rid of.

Punishment

Punishment as psychologists in my field define it is very different from the term as used in everyday life, in both the what (definition) and the how (when and how it's delivered). As a technical term, *punishment refers solely to presentation or removal of events after a behavior that reduces the probability or likelihood of that behavior occurring in the future.* In our programs at the Yale Parenting Center, punishment is used to decrease some behavior, and that's it. But in everyday life, punishment has many other agendas. In child rearing, teaching, law enforcement, and other pursuits, we punish not only to change behavior but also to serve justice by trying to make the consequence fit the crime, inspire remorse, teach a moral lesson, or send a message. Many of these other motives are worthwhile and even admirable, but they can get in the way of improving behavior. It's often the case that parents (and teachers, and the legal system) end up pursuing multiple (and often vaguely defined) goals at cross-purposes when they try to use punishment to *both* change behavior *and* impart other lessons. I fully understand that you may want to use punishment to send a message, teach a lesson, and so on, but if you really want to change your child's behavior, make that your priority, which means conceiving of and using punishment in a different way. Sending messages, teaching lessons, teachable moments—these are all wonderful parenting clichés of our time, but not effective strategies for developing behavior.

It's a useful exercise to ask yourself at the moment before you punish, "What's my main goal here? Do I want to make a statement of some kind by showing that this behavior cannot be tolerated in this home, that people do not do this, and so on; or do I want to make this behavior not occur in the future?" These different goals usually call for different actions. The desire to make a statement tends to lead to stark dramatic punishment—shouting, stern reprimands, anger—followed with an explanation along the lines of "What if everybody acted like that?" or "If you do that, the world will think you are a complete jerk." If you want to change behavior, you will respond differently; think first of building up the positive opposite, and use very gentle punishment, if any.

I de-emphasize punishment in our programs for five reasons:

1. Punishment does not teach a child positive behaviors to engage in. Getting rid of what you do not want does not immediately put into the child's repertoire what you want (positive opposite), even if the child understands what to do. For example, either in a very admirable and measured way or after blowing up spectacularly, you may tell your child not to be so rough when playing with the baby because the baby is young and can easily get hurt. Your child may listen to this and even give you a reassuring nod to show that he understands, and he probably does understand. Unfortunately, that may not change his behavior at all. Instead, reinforce your child for being gentle with the baby.

2. Punishment is not very effective. Yes, it may well suppress behavior immediately—a shout, a slap, a loud reprimand is often temporarily effective right at the moment it occurs. But the science on this shows clearly that the rate of the problem behavior (the number of times it happens each day, each week, each month) does not change with punishment, even though you witnessed an immediate change at the moment you punished. So the behavior keeps happening and you

keep punishing—and, to make matters worse, the natural human tendency is for the punishment to escalate as the child adjusts to it. So now you have to punish a lot more to get that initial immediate pause in the behavior, and it's still going to come back as often as ever. Children adapt to that more intense punishment so that it has no stronger an effect than the less intense punishment.

3. Alternative procedures such as positive reinforcement can often be used to achieve the same goal as punishment—namely, to decrease or eliminate a behavior—and without punishment's side effects. So reinforcement of positive opposites is much more effective than any of the punishment options. For example, as your frequently misbehaving child walks down the aisle of the grocery store and does not touch items on the shelves, you say, "Great! You kept your hands to yourself and didn't touch anything on the shelves as we just walked down this aisle!" (Now do a quick touch.) That will work wonders, and you can pair that with occasional very mild reprimands when he does touch items on the shelves, as long as you praise the desired behavior more frequently than you punish the undesired behavior.

4. Punishment often is associated with undesirable side effects such as emotional reactions (crying), escape and avoidance (for example, staying away from a punitive parent), and aggression (such as hitting others, including you). Also, shouting at, reprimanding, or shaking the child can get the child very upset, but don't mistake that reaction for a sign that the child's behavior will improve. Some side effects go beyond just getting upset. For example, moderate to frequent spanking (a few times a month) helps make a child more aggressive. Parents often take these side effects (especially crying) as a sign that punishment must be working, but in fact these effects have almost nothing to do with getting the behavior to stop.

5. Punishment can inspire undesirable associations with various people (parents, teachers), situations (home, school), and

behaviors (doing homework) that are important for a child. A vital objective in rearing a well-socialized child is to foster positive attitudes toward these important people, situations, and behaviors; their frequent association with punishment makes it harder to achieve that objective. For example, parents often think their adolescents can talk to them about anything, but teens often avoid parents because they fear reprimands and judgment, to which teens are especially sensitive. This is especially harmful when they avoid parents on important but touchy topics, like peer relations, sex, and substance use.

So why even talk about punishment? Well, it *is* used often in everyday life, frequently in ways that are ineffective and can actually do harm, principally via side effects. Also, there is a genuine role for punishment in an effective program for changing behavior, and clarifying that role can improve your effectiveness as a parent. In addition, I recognize that parents don't just respond to behavior. It's likely that you punish for all kinds of reasons that go well beyond changing behavior, so you might as well know how punishment affects behavior.

Your punishment toolkit

There are three broad categories of punishment: things you present to the child, things you take away, and things you require your child to do.

Things you present to the child, the technical term for which is *aversive consequences:* shouting, reprimands, threats, and other responses that the child dislikes and would rather avoid (so, the negative opposite of a reward). This category embraces everything from a warning look (which, used properly, can work very well) to counting to three (less effective) to hauling off and belting a child (which won't do any good and which I would never endorse). They're all grouped together because if you're trying to improve behavior, the threat of such a punishment *is* a punishment. Parents do not need research to prove that this kind of punishment, when it's the primary means of trying to improve behavior, is not effective beyond the immediate moment. The reason parents find themselves saying things like "If I have told you once, I have told you a thousand times" is that scolding, threatening, raising a hand to warn of an impending blow, the blow itself, and all other aversive consequences are ineffective when it comes to permanently reducing or eliminating a behavior. In fact, frequent reprimands have been shown to actually make an undesirable behavior happen *more* frequently. So if this is your favored method for dealing with misbehavior, get used to doing it all the time, and be prepared for your child to adapt to the punishment faster than you can escalate it, a nasty household arms race that's both unnecessary and harmful to all.

Things you take away, or *withdrawal of positive events,* meaning time out, removing a point if a point chart is being used, and other methods of taking away something the child likes and wants. The most common version is time out, which psychologists call by its more precise name: *time out from reinforcement,* which refers to *withdrawal of a positive reinforcer for a certain period of time.* During the time-out interval, the child does not have access to the positive reinforcers that are normally available in the setting. For example, a child may be isolated from others in class for ten minutes. During that time she will not interact with peers or have access to activities, privileges, or the teacher's attention.

Time out can be very brief to be effective. Just the first minute or couple of minutes does the work of changing behavior. More time out does not make it more effective, and more than about ten minutes can begin to have negative side effects. The child can sit on a chair, go to his room, or sit in a special place where he can be supervised but doesn't receive attention. Time out has nothing to do with contemplating one's sins or considering what might have been done better. It works on pigeons, rats, and other animals incapable of moral reflection, and it works the same way on children — and adults, for that matter. (I am not saying that your child resembles even the cutest rat or pigeon in any way, but think about this: a ball, a shoe, and a feather don't resemble each other, but it's fair to say that gravity works on all of them. And so with your future Nobel laureate of a child, who responds to time out and gravity in the same ways that all sorts of living things do.)

The effectiveness of time out depends on a brief, temporary loss of access to the usual reinforcers, and that's all. The crucial ingredient is delineating a brief period during which reinforcement is unavailable. Ideally, during this period *all* sources of reinforcement are withdrawn. This ideal is not always attainable. For example, if a child is sent to her room as punishment, removal from the existing sources of reinforcement qualifies as time out. However, all reinforcement may not be withheld; she may engage in a number of reinforcing activities such as playing a computer game, listening to music, or sleeping. Despite these possibilities, sending her to her room will do if it's the only option. Better would be sitting on a chair or couch or in a corner for just a brief period.

Time out usually removes an individual from the situation. But sometimes, if the child can't be removed, reinforcers available in the setting can be stopped for a brief period. One variation of time out is called *planned ignoring,* a period of time in which the parent, teacher, or other person makes no reinforcing contact with the child. This would include no comments, eye contact, nonverbal pats, or praise. Here is a good use of planned ignoring: Say your three-year-old child occasionally hits you. After you are hit, you ignore the child for one or two minutes. Before, you would have attended to her, grabbed her hand, and said, "You do not hit Mommy!"—all behaviors that are likely not to work, at best, and, at worst, to increase hitting in the future. When you respond with planned ignoring, after the child hits you, you stay in the room, but for two minutes you make no eye contact and you don't talk to or interact with the child for this brief time period. This is "time out" because the child has no access to your attention. After the time elapses, you resume all of your usual activities with the child. This is one example where the child receives time out but is not isolated or excluded physically from the situation.

In a nutshell, time out should be

- Used sparingly, because the side effects of excessive punishment are more significant than any benefits the time out might have. If you're giving more than one or two per day for the same offense, that's too much.
- Brief, because the time out's positive effect on behavior is almost all concentrated in its first minute or two. Some parents feel obliged to add more time to satisfy their sense of justice, but the extra time has no value in terms of changing behavior. If you feel that you must go beyond one or two minutes, treat ten minutes as the extreme upper limit.
- Immediate, following as closely as possible upon the behavior that made it necessary. If you can, do it on the spot, not when you get home from the store or playground. Delayed time out is ineffective.
- Done in isolation from others, with the child in a separate room or sitting alone in a chair off to one side. Complete isolation is not needed if you feel it would be good to keep an eye on the child.
- Administered calmly, not in anger or as an act of vengeance, and without repeated warnings, which lose their effect if they are not regularly followed with consequences. Make clear to the child which behaviors led to time out, and then be consistent about declaring one when such behavior occurs. One warning is plenty. Later in this chapter I will say more about how to make time out effective, including the less familiar but vitally important concept of "time in."

Withdrawing privileges is another familiar punishment often used in the home. You temporarily take away something the child likes to do or is granted routinely—TV time, use of a cell phone or bicycle, time with friends, and so on. This approach can be effective, but only if you keep two important principles in mind when you use it.

First, the child should know ahead of time exactly what the penalty is, well before you invoke it. In the usual home situation, the parent wings it on the spot: "What did you just say to me? That's it, we're giving away your dog and I'm not paying for college!" Shooting from the hip like that, being arbitrary or appearing to be arbitrary, is a setting event for your child to have tantrums, get upset, and otherwise make a scene. And punishment improvised on the spot is not only likely to appear arbitrary and unfair but also to be more severe than punishment that was planned in advance, all of which leads to more side effects. So specify in advance what privileges will be taken away and for how long; then invoke the punishment, if necessary, calmly and without unnecessary drama.

Second, brevity is the key when withdrawing privileges. I know you're tempted to declare, "You can't use your bike for two weeks!" This is not necessary—one or two days maximum would have the same effect, since the behavior-changing power of the consequence lies in the initial moment of taking away a privilege, not in the long duration of its removal. I know that one or two days may not feel like a punishment that adequately fits the crime, and from the standpoint of justice you may well be right. But it's all that's necessary to change behavior. Also, a bicycle is often a source of contact with peers that usually we want to foster. Try to find another way to satisfy the demands of justice.

Things you require your child to do: work or activity that the child regards as unpleasant. If you use this consequence, the chore should be brief. Here, too, requiring more effort—more time weeding the garden, more time cleaning the garage—does not increase the effectiveness of punishment. The required work can be unrelated to the offense being punished, like having to stack firewood for using bad language, or related to the offense, like cleaning up and fixing vandalism done to a school building.

Effects of punishment

Immediacy of effects. This is a tricky notion because it has two meanings. First, the punishment (shout, threat) may stop the behavior in the moment. Even a stark punishment with major negative side effects—like a slap in the face, which of course I would never condone—will interrupt the behavior. This immediate but short-lived effect causes a parent to fall into what is called the "punishment trap." The momentary success of the punishment unwittingly reinforces the person delivering punishment (you) and *develops the habit further in the parent.*

Here's how it works. The child is doing something annoying, the parent shouts or pounds the table, the child's inappropriate behavior stops. This is a type of reinforcement of the parent that locks in shouting or whatever the punishment was. That is, the immediate effectiveness locks in parent behavior; the delayed ineffectiveness of the punishment, which does nothing to decrease recurrences of the bad behavior, has no real impact on the parent's tendency to punish. For example, I have worked with many parents who abuse their children—I mean that their punishments rise above the line drawn by the law to define child abuse—and they know it's not working but they do it anyway. They've been seduced and trapped by the immediate but temporary cessation of the child's misbehavior that happens right at the moment they punish.

The second meaning of "immediacy of effects" is that if punishment is going to have any longer-term effect, more than just interrupting a behavior at that moment, this effect should start to be evident soon—like, in a couple of days. A punishment-centered behavior-change program usually won't work at all, but if it does work, you would see a slight decrease in the behavior in the first few days. Let me be clear about what this means: the behavior doesn't just temporarily stop at the moment you punish; it recurs less often. This doesn't have to be a large decrease, but it should be at least a discernible trend. If you don't see the improvement right away, you can conclude that punishment isn't going to work. I mention this because more than one parent has said to me something like "I'm going to keep punishing him"—in one case hitting, in another case holding the child by the shoulders and shaking—"until he gets the message and stops hitting other kids." Chances are that the child will get the message, which is "me hitting usually leads to my dad shaking me," but this punishment will not be more effective over time. Knowing, understanding, and grasping the message will not change behavior and certainly will not develop the positive (opposite) behavior you wish for your child.

Bottom line: Punishment is not likely to work, but if it is going to work, you will see an inkling of the effects right away. Even if you do see that improvement, bear in mind that the punishment is likely to get less rather than more effective over time in light of this next characteristic.

Recovery from punishment. Again, the most critical point is that punishment usually does not have the enduring effect of reducing and eliminating behavior. But sometimes it does have a very different enduring effect, one that's bad for both child and parent. What happens is that the child adapts to the punishment, the technical term for which is *recovery from punishment*. The punishment continues when the behavior occurs but loses its effects as the child adapts to the punishment, causing the unwanted behavior to go back to its pre-punishment rate. This adaptation to punishment often leads the parent to escalate: instead of shouting, much harsher shouting and a threat; instead of one blow, a few blows; instead of hitting with a hand, hitting with a belt. Most parents do not go to the highest level of escalation, but a surprising number escalate well beyond any level they intended to reach or feel comfortable reaching. They sink deeper into the punishment trap because more and more severe punishment continues to stop the behavior for the moment.

Undesirable side effects. Punishment can have many undesirable side effects. They're called side effects because they're not related to the goals of punishment or to whether punishment even is working. The irony of all of this is that even when punishment is not working, the side effects emerge. Medicines come to market because their therapeutic effects (how they help the problem) are worthwhile despite side effects (consequences that are annoying, painful, or even dangerous).

Punishment that doesn't work is like chemotherapy that makes your hair fall out and makes you nauseous but has no effect on cancer.

The side effects of punishment include the following:

Emotional reactions: being upset, crying, begging, and so on. Parents sometimes even say, "You *ought to* be upset!" Seeing the child's emotional upset also contributes to the punishment trap by suggesting to the parent that the punishment is working, that it fit the crime, or that a lesson is being learned. Yet whether the child is upset or not is unrelated to the effectiveness of punishment. Getting your child to cry, wail, plead for mercy while crying—none of this is related to behavior change.

Escape and avoidance. A child will seek to get away from a person (parent, teacher) or a situation (school, dinnertime at home) that is frequently associated with punishment. If a child wants to escape from or avoid parents or teachers, he'll be less likely to seek out these adults in time of need—when he has a problem, when he needs counsel or understanding. The opposite of avoidance is approach, and children are less likely to approach adults who punish relatively frequently—here, "relatively" means in relation to how much positive reinforcement that adult gives them. Also, we want to be sure the child does not wish to escape from situations (for example, home, classroom) that should be associated with comfort, learning, and other major positives. When something leads to escape, it has become aversive. Punishing a child for, say, not practicing an instrument can backfire on a parent because it can make an otherwise positive experience or activity truly aversive.

Aggression. Punishment sometimes results in aggressive behavior, usually against the person who is delivering punishment. If you hit or spank a child, the likelihood of being hit back is pretty high. Once that occurs (and no parent can take that calmly), punishment usually escalates. Even with a punishment as mild as time out, here is a common scenario: The parent tells the child to go to her room for a few minutes of time out. The child says no. Now the parent may forcibly take the child to time out—grabbing and lifting the child, forcibly walking the child to time out. This is almost a guarantee that the child will flail with her arms and hit the parent. The parent usually then increases the force of his grip, resulting in more aggressive behavior and a cascade of emotional effects to go along with an increase in the child's aggression.

So what should the parent do when the child refuses time out? Have a backup plan set in advance, such as taking away a privilege. So you say, "Go to your room for five minutes of time out." The child says, "No, I won't." You then give one—just one—warning: "Once more, I am asking you to go to time out." If the child still refuses, then no warnings, no lectures, no tirades on your part. You just say, "OK, you lose TV privileges tonight" or whatever else you had decided in advance would be the lost privilege. And you walk away—calmly, not in a hot or cold fury, not as if making a dramatic exit—to avoid the ensuing back-and-forth.

It's important that you work out in advance what the penalty will be, and that you tell your child in advance whenever possible. When you specify a punishment in advance, you can include punishment options you wish to retain: "If you don't go straight into time out when I tell you to, you will lose a privilege that will either be TV for the day or computer time for the day." But it's even better to name just one punishment and to be specific about it. The main reason is that if parents have worked out an explicit punishment ahead of time and have laid things out for their child in advance, they are less likely to wing it on the spot when the offense happens. In the heat of the moment, with everyone yelling and angry, winging it is risky because your reaction is likely to be more severe and arbitrary, as in "That's it, you just lost your favorite doll FOR THE REST OF YOUR LIFE!" The greater severity is likely to produce more side effects without any benefit in behavior change. The arbitrariness will be an antecedent for the child's negative reaction (not just side effects) because she feels she has no real say, control, or choice in anything in the home. As setting events go, "arbitrary" can be considered the opposite of choice. When you take away a predetermined, known, reasonably chosen privilege in a calm way, rather than reacting excitedly in the heat of the moment, your reasonableness and consistency in keeping to a plan will positively influence your child's behavior and compliance beyond this particular incident.

Modeled punishment. When you punish, you're modeling punishment for your child. We know from research that children "discipline" their peers in the same ways their parents discipline them. This is not a problem if you punish in moderation, but it can become one if you go overboard. That's one of the reasons that the most aggressive children are those whose parents hit them a lot. So when you punish, you are doing more than using a procedure that is likely to be ineffective—you're teaching a way of interacting with others. Moderation, restraint, and lots of positive reinforcement for positive opposite behavior mitigate all of this.

How to use punishment so it actually works

1. The single most important factor in using punishment is that, whatever punishment is used, it must play a minor role in the behavior-change program. The effectiveness of punishment depends on whether and how often the positive opposite is reinforced. Punishment by itself is a losing battle. It just doesn't teach the behaviors you want, and without that, a strategy of suppressing little instances of the behavior here and there does not work beyond the moment. But punishment is not useless; the research shows that a strong reinforcement program can be enhanced by very occasional punishment when the child doesn't do the behavior you're trying to develop.

By way of illustration, take time out, a popular punishment that virtually everyone knows about. The effectiveness of time out depends on what you do during "time in," which refers to all the time that the child is not in time out. If the desirable behavior is consistently and frequently rewarded during time in, a well-used time out will help develop the behavior you want. As a guide, for every time the child is placed in time out, be sure the positive opposite behavior is reinforced four or five times more during time in. Reinforced practice of the desired behavior is the guiding concept of the approach; punishment on its own will not teach the child what to do.

Bottom line: There is no such thing in this book as a punishment program. There is a positive reinforcement program that includes occasional and mild punishment as a component. Also, positive reinforcement supplemented by punishment is much less likely to have the undesirable side effects associated with punishment alone. The positive reinforcement leads to all sorts of more positive side effects — good emotional reactions, more cooperative rather than aggressive behavior, a stronger bond between parent and child.

2. Keep punishment mild. Making the punishment fit the crime may well make sense from some perspectives (like a desire to instill an appreciation of justice), but not from the standpoint of changing behavior. So your child stays out past her curfew and you are thinking, "Do I take away her iPad and cell phone for a week or two, or just a day or two?" The offense seems to deserve a week or two, and a day or two feels to you as if she's getting off too lightly. Yet, the day or two will have the maximum effect on changing behavior. More is not better in punishment, because more is not more effective and it produces more bad side effects. Mild punishment can be effective when strong positive reinforcement is in place around it. What that means is that a disapproving look, a few minutes of time out, or saying, "No, don't do that" would virtually never work as a stand-alone punishment program, yet when built into a reinforcement program, these and other forms of mild punishment can help change behavior.

3. Do not use as punishing consequences any activities you want your child to like. Some traditional school punishments violate this principle. Common examples include doing extra homework, having to read more in an assigned book, staying after school, staying in class during recess, writing an essay about why the behavior was wrong, or writing "I will not . . ." over and over on the board à la Bart Simpson.

Short of corporal punishment, these are the worst possible punishing consequences. We want children to have a positive attitude toward homework, books, staying in school, and so on. Staying after school could easily be a reward if you set it up right; we want being in class to be desired; and we never want reading and writing to be associated with punishment. At home the same problem can emerge if a parent punishes a child by having him work on reading, practice an instrument, or sit with a parent (so he can be monitored and controlled better). Most parents do not want reading, practicing, or being with them to become negative—so if you use an activity as punishment, give some thought to choosing one that doesn't attach an aversive association to something you actually want your child to do or like.

At home, there are additional examples of punishments one ought to be cautious about using. For example, a commonly used punishment is taking away some privilege for a while: "You can't use your bike for two weeks"; "You're grounded and can't have activities with friends for a month"; and so on. This seems innocuous enough, but it's counterproductive. We want the child to socialize with peers, and bike riding and going out with friends (if safe and otherwise fine) are good for the child. Here is a case where taking away the privilege might be effective but the duration of the consequence is questionable. If your child rides her bike every day, two days of taking away the bike is plenty. There's no added benefit to piling on more days or weeks. A steeper penalty does not have a stronger impact on children's behavior.

Bottom line: Devote your principal energy to positively reinforcing the positive opposites; if you do punish, do it mildly and don't use a behavior you want as a punishment.

4. When punishment is used as part of a reinforcement program, it should be delivered immediately after the behavior. If the purpose is changing behavior, delayed punishment—"When we get home you're going to be sorry," or "Yesterday you teased the cat, so today you can't go out and play"—isn't worth the trouble.

5. Punish consistently and try to catch all or most instances of misbehavior with the punishment you selected. Punishing irregularly, catching the behavior a few times and letting other instances go, is doomed to failure. No matter how many times you punish behavior, be sure the positive opposite is reinforced for many more instances. Otherwise you basically have a punishment program, and be prepared for that to be ineffective and frustrating.

6. Behaviors you want to eliminate often have positive reinforcement associated with them. Ask yourself, when the child does this unwanted behavior, "Is there a response that makes it likely to happen again?" If that's the case, punishment is not likely to work. Here's why: the annoying behavior is immediately reinforced, and punishment after that sequence won't undo that chain. For example, in a class, if when a child shouts out even just one peer laughs or smiles or gives some attention, the child's shouting is being reinforced by his peers. The teacher might jump in immediately and say, "Two minutes of time out for you," but it's too late; the behavior has already been reinforced. Punishment will not work if reinforcement for the behavior is squeezed in first.

Delayed negative consequences do not overcome immediate reinforcing consequences. A child who takes another's lunch money, for instance, experiences immediate reinforcement of his act. He gets both the money and the frightened victim's submissiveness, a powerful cocktail of rewards. Any negative consequences will be delayed; eventually he may get caught and perhaps punished with detention or suspension, and his crimes may someday pull him into a long-term engagement with the legal system that impinges on his life chances in all sorts of ways. But those delayed consequences don't exert a strong influence for many reasons, key among which is that delayed punishment doesn't break the powerful behavior-building sequence of lunch-money theft followed by immediate reinforcement. In a different universe in which the consequences were reversed, as soon as the lunch-money thief said, "Gimme your lunch money," he would suffer all the consequences that normally take years and even decades to show up: horrible pangs of remorse, existential despair, instantaneous teleportation to lockup in juvie and then the adult penitentiary, and a terrible beating or two from the fellow criminals he will eventually encounter there. Then, weeks, months, years later, he'd get the delayed rewards: a couple of dollars and the pleasure of his victim's submissive response to him. In that universe, stealing lunch money would not be reinforced, and he'd stop doing it right away. But that's not the way it works.

Remember the punishment trap, when a parent's habit of punishing the child gets locked in? That's another case in which the immediate consequences (the child stops misbehaving the moment she's punished) control the parent's behavior, even though the delayed consequences (in the hours and days that follow) show that the behavior has not changed at all—it still happens just as often. The parents who come to the Yale Parenting Center often recognize the delayed consequences; they know their constant punishment isn't working. But their recognition that what they're doing is failing in the long run is not as strong an influence on their behavior as immediate reinforcement. That's what makes it a trap. The punishment continues or even increases even though no one (child, parent, teacher) believes it's working.

Bottom line: Ask yourself, "When the child does this disruptive behavior, what happens?" Is the "what happens" something that might help maintain the behavior? If so, try to break the connection. That can be hard to do; it's one of the reasons that reinforcing positive opposites is so important and so effective. You might not be able to stop others from attending to some disruptive behavior, but developing positive opposites will give them fewer opportunities to attend to it.

Punishment as a secondary part of a reinforcement program

There are four interrelated reasons why reinforcement should be the primary element of a program that also uses punishment:

- Positive reinforcement for alternative behavior increases the effectiveness of punishment, making it more effective in quickly and thoroughly reducing unwanted behavior. You can compensate for many limitations of punishment by providing reinforcers for alternative or other positive behaviors.
- Reinforcement can develop appropriate behaviors to displace the inappropriate behaviors that are to be eliminated. This is important because, while punishment can help to eliminate behaviors, it's not effective in building new ones.
- When you're positively reinforcing alternative behavior, less severe punishments are likely to be more effective than would otherwise be the case. Mildly aversive events that normally would have little or no effect—a grimace, calmly saying no—are much more likely to be effective in a richly reinforcing environment.
- Finally, positive reinforcement combined with punishment can reduce or eliminate undesirable side effects that might result from the use of punishment alone. Milder and fewer punishments are likely to be needed with positive reinforcement in place for developing prosocial behavior.

One parent at the Yale Parenting Center had an eight-year-old who constantly resisted her instructions. He just said, "No, I won't" to all sorts of routine requests: Get dressed so we can go, get ready for bed, come down to breakfast, finish eating your vegetables, and so on. She thought she was not being consistent in handling these situations, so she began punishing each instance with a very loud shout; she never hit the child, but occasionally she would slap the table with a flat hand to accompany the shout with a loud noise and aggressive gesture.

A little background is relevant. The mother had been divorced for eight months when she came to us. She and her son lived alone, and the boy made weekly overnight visits to his father. The divorce had two likely effects. First, children (and parents, too) often show disturbances in behavior—more psychological problems, stress reactions, moodiness, and the like—during that period of adjustment after any shakeup like a loss, move, or divorce. Even positive events, like the birth of a sibling, can have such effects. They're likely to go away on their own, but it may take some time. The child's behavior, and perhaps the mother's behavior as well, might temporarily be different from what it was and will soon be. Second, the mother now had a much more stressful life. In addition to her high-powered job as a prosecuting attorney, she had sole responsibility for all of the tasks that had been partially shared—paying bills, handling daycare—and now some new ones, like negotiating custody arrangements with her ex. When her child was sick or when daycare arrangements after school collapsed for some reason, the mother was on her own to manage it all. All of this led her to feel very stressed, which she recognized. We already know from chapter one that stress on a parent can contribute to a child's noncompliance because it affects tone of voice, level of urgency, the parent's willingness to give a choice, and other factors that influence the likelihood that a request will get the desired response. This is not about fault; it's about how we can effectively mobilize ABCs to change behavior.

We began the program exactly the way I hope you are thinking we did—with positive opposites. What behavior did the mom want? She wanted her son to do what she asked "without any lip" (her term). We asked the mom to "catch" all instances in which he did comply with a request—she had indicated that there were some, but it was clear that she really attended to and responded to the instances when he refused. We conveyed that the instances when he did do what he was asked were the ones to care about, take notice of, and praise. We practiced the praise in two separate sessions. She still felt he should be punished when he didn't do what he was asked to do, so we included a brief, nonverbal, disapproving look. Specifically, the mom was to shake her head back and forth (as if saying no with body English) and then purse her lips as part of the disapproving grimace. This was to be very brief (left, right, left head turn, count to three and no more). The main program was, of course, reinforcement of the desired behavior. That program would probably work all by itself, but we were also shaping the mom to use milder punishment. Also, as the research shows, if you're pursuing a strong positive reinforcement program, introducing occasional mild punishment (a look, mild disapproval) can speed the process a little—not a lot, but just a little.

We asked the mom to praise as many instances of compliance as she could and not to give the disapproving look more than two or three times per day. We added some antecedents to take the tone and stress out of the instructions to the child: we practiced using "please" first and having the mother smile a bit more when giving instructions. Both of these were likely to take the edge off of the instructions and so help compliance.

Within nine days, the child complied with almost all requests. The mother was really surprised and credited us with the change. But of course all the changes were made by her. While her son did not comply every single time, there was no more battle of wills. We also conveyed that it would still be good to praise compliance once in a while with words and hugs, especially if it was something especially difficult for the child or a request that he had not complied with recently. Also, we reminded her that it is common, normative, and very human for children (and adults) not to comply 100 percent of the time, and it would be unrealistic and unfair to expect anything close to that. We checked on progress, and after a while the program (praise and disapproving looks) dropped out because it was no longer necessary: noncompliance was not an issue.

During one of our follow-up calls we asked her about her punishment practices more generally and what she was doing. She laughed over the phone and said, "It's all about positive opposites! Were you trying to trick me with that question?"

To punish or not to punish?

The research shows us that punishment is wildly overrated and overused as a way of changing behavior, and not among the most useful tools in a parent's toolkit, but the science does not quite support being categorically opposed to it. When used properly, even just a mild look of disapproval can be punishment, and it can be a useful adjunct to change behavior.

Many of my fellow professionals *are* categorically against punishing children, but most of their concerns are in relation to spanking and hitting children and extend beyond the purely scientific into the moral and legal realms. For example, it's usually against the law for one adult to hit another. Violation of the law has penalties, like going to jail. Yet in most countries there is no parallel law that protects the child in this way.

Once one throws out spanking and other aggressive forms of punishment—threatening, shouting, and so forth—and moves to milder punishments like calm reprimands or briefly isolating a child in his room, many of the objections subside, and that's where I see an acceptable place for punishment as part of a larger program to change behavior. But let me underscore that the science doesn't show any value at all in hitting children, and it does show that physical punishment, even when moderate and not abusive, can have long-term negative consequences for physical health (it's associated with more illnesses, earlier than usual death in adulthood), mental health (higher rates of psychiatric disorder in adulthood), and academic problems (children do more poorly in school and drop out of high school at higher rates). And yet research on the United States shows that everyday methods of punishment still include spanking for most children.

I advise against severe punishment and any punishment program that isn't associated with a strong reinforcement program for positive opposites. Punishment by itself is not likely to work and has all sorts of side effects, including harming relationships. Also, as we've seen, there is a tendency to escalate ineffective punishment. And I want to caution you against wasting your efforts on any punishment that is ineffective, even if it is mild, because it displaces effective procedures you could be using to make the changes you would like in your child's behavior.

Yet, research supports the view that when there's a positive reinforcement program to develop behavior, very mild punishment can help. A brief time out, a mild reprimand, some corrective feedback, a brief loss of a privilege—these can help a program work, as long as the emphasis is on positive reinforcement and punishment is an adjunct to this program.

Dos

- Think of the positive opposite whenever there is some annoying, disturbing, or otherwise undesirable behavior you want to eliminate. That's always the first step. Specify that behavior as a starting point to develop a reinforcement program.
- Develop a plan for how to reinforce the behavior. Maybe shaping or a simulation (chapter two) is needed. But what behavior will be reinforced and what reinforcer will be used? Praise is the default reinforcer because it can be so effective when delivered correctly.
- Employ a mild form of punishment.
- Accept that effective punishment will probably not fit the crime.
- Keep in mind that punishment by itself, severe or mild, is not likely to work beyond the moment in changing behavior. Reinforcing positive opposites is always key.
- Bear in mind that punishment is secondary to a reinforcement program; once a reinforcement program is in place, mild punishment can be effective as an adjunct.
- Be sure that instances of reinforcing the positive far outnumber instances of administering the mild punishment on any given day.

Don'ts

- Don't waste your creativity on coming up with novel ways to punish misbehavior.
- Don't believe for a moment that you are teaching a lesson or sending a message by rapid punishment of some act. Punishment does not teach what to do, and without teaching that, the effects on what not to do are extremely short-lived.
- Don't believe that knowing and doing are necessarily related. A

lot of parents tell me something like "My child needs to know that such behavior will not be tolerated in this house." That is fine as a statement, and I expect that your child, if she's old enough to discuss it, knows the rule. But knowing and understanding the rule by itself will not lead to your child changing the behavior. Bottom line: To teach knowing and understanding, talk about the rules, especially when everyone is calm. Look for opportunities to point out examples of following the rules if you see something on TV, in a store, at the mall. Say to your child, "Look how that boy is playing so nicely with his baby sister." But bear in mind that none of the above will be sufficient to get the behavior you want. Don't confuse ways of imparting knowledge with ways of changing behavior. Imparting knowledge is a useful first step, but the first step by itself does not get up the stairs to the behaviors you want. You still need reinforced practice and positive opposites for that.

Withholding reinforcement

Many unwanted behaviors are maintained by consequences that follow from them. For example, temper tantrums and interrupting others during conversations are often unwittingly reinforced by a parent's attention. When you're trying to reduce a behavior, not paying attention to it can help by eliminating the connection between the behavior and the consequences that follow.

Often, an unwanted behavior may have received some reinforcer—for instance, when a child talks back, she gets lots of attention from a parent in the form of lectures, yelling, and other engagement. Withholding reinforcement means that the behavior (talking back, in this case) no longer receives that reinforcer (parental attention in any form), and it eventually decreases in frequency.

For example, when you're trying to start your car, the behavior (turning the key, pressing a pedal) is usually followed by the reinforcing consequence (car starting). But when your car is not working, your behavior of repeatedly turning the key stops pretty quickly after several unsuccessful attempts. Similarly, you may warmly greet a particular stranger whom you pass each day. Your behavior (saying hello and smiling) may be followed by positive reinforcement (acknowledgment and a similar greeting by the other person). If the other person's responses were no longer forthcoming, your behavior would be likely to decrease and perhaps cease. When the reinforcement that followed your behavior is no longer forthcoming, you're likely to do less of that behavior.

A typical example from the Yale Parenting Center was Danica, a four-year-old girl who played with her food at the dinner table. She made shapes of things on her plate or picked up some food with a utensil, raised the utensil high, and dropped the food back on her plate, and she also spit out food while blurting out something she wanted to say. Invariably, her parents were right there with something corrective: "Don't play with your food; finish chewing and swallowing before you talk," and so on. This corrective action was intended as punishment, but it was also attention for behaviors the parents wanted to get rid of.

Yes, negative attention can be a positive reinforcer for behavior. This is one reason why we make a distinction between rewards (something the recipient subjectively values or likes) and reinforcers. Probably no one on the planet would say that a reprimand is a reward, but because it entails paying attention to the child, it can reinforce a behavior.

As part of a program to decrease Danica's annoying and messy behaviors at the table, we began to break the connection between her misbehavior and her parents' pattern of paying attention to her. We wanted to reorient their displays of purposeful attention to moments when she was behaving in ways they approved of, ways they wanted to reinforce. As I'll explain later, programs of withholding reinforcement are not very effective by themselves, so the program was also part of—you guessed it—reinforcing positive opposites: eating correctly, speaking with no food in her mouth, and so on.

Your withholding reinforcement toolkit

Because many behaviors are maintained by attention, the most common variation of withholding reinforcement is no longer paying attention to the behavior. This means looking away from the child or not making eye contact when she engages in the behavior. The tricky part is that sometimes the child's behavior is maintained by a reinforcer that's different from the one you've identified.

For example, in the case of Danica, the four-year-old with terrible table manners, the mother and father provided attention, and we thought that might well be the unintended reinforcer. But the rest of the story was very relevant. Danica had twin older brothers, age six, who were raucously amused at Danica's food behavior. They laughed each time her food splatted back onto the plate. One liked to wipe his forehead, laughing, as if her food had hit him. This sibling attention could have been the reinforcer maintaining the behavior, by itself or along with parental attention. Withholding reinforcement means no longer providing the reinforcer that is maintaining the behavior, but you have to be sure about the reinforcer to target.

We needed a two-pronged program. First, of course, we wanted a reinforcement program of positive opposites. The parents praised Danica at least three times during a meal for appropriate use of food and utensils. We specified praising at least three times, rather than "when you see it or when you can," as a concrete guide to help them. (There's no research specifying that praising three times per meal is a magic number. We just wanted to make it clear that reinforcing the positive opposite should happen a lot more than punishing the unwanted behavior, and we specified a number of times to help them remember to praise and to redirect their attention away from looking out for misbehavior. Praising good behavior four or five times per meal would be even better.)

Second, we wanted to remove sibling attention and laughing. To address that, we had the parents institute a group dessert program. The children were told that at the end of dinner there would be a dessert they could choose from between two options. They would get the dessert if Danica did not play with her food *or* if Danica played with her food but the brothers did not laugh or react in any way. The mother had the idea of putting the dessert on the counter, conspicuously visible from the kitchen table. This was clever on her part because seeing the reinforcer that can be earned is an antecedent (setting event) that increases the likelihood of getting the behavior. A shaping nuance: we suggested that the dessert-earning program at first not be for the whole meal—that is, we suggested breaking the time period of the meal into halves, and shaping more and more time of sibling behavior. Thus, at first if Danica did not play with food for the second fifteen minutes (second half of dinner) or her brothers didn't laugh if she did, the dessert would be earned. We chose the second half because that would make dessert—the reinforcer—immediately follow the desired behavior, and immediacy makes the program much more effective. If we chose the first half, that might have worked, too, but there would be a delay between great first-half behavior and the reinforcer.

Once this partial program was succeeding regularly, the parents could move to making good first- and second-half periods a requirement for earning dessert. The mother thought it would be easier just to include the whole meal, so she started with that. No harm done. If the whole-meal plan failed, if it turned out that the children weren't ready to do the full set of good behaviors required for the dessert, it would be easy to switch to the shaping plan. It turned out the mother was right. The full-meal plan worked, dessert was regularly earned, and most importantly, sibling consequences that helped maintain playing with food were eliminated.

Withholding reinforcement was also used in one study to reduce awakening in the middle of the night among infants. Nighttime waking, evident in 20 to 50 percent of infants, can be a significant problem for parents. And yet parents may play a role in sustaining night waking by attending to the infant in ways that reinforce the behavior. In the study, waking up during the night was defined as a sustained noise (more than a minute) from the infant between onset of sleep and an agreed-upon waking time in the morning. After measuring wakings for each infant, parents were instructed to no longer give attention to night wakings. If the parent had any concern about the health or safety of the child, the parent was told to enter the room, check the child quietly and in silence with a minimum of light, and leave immediately if there was no problem. This practice of withholding reinforcement led to a dramatic decrease in night wakings. The program was ended, and evaluation three months and then two years later showed that wakings were no longer a problem.

Characteristics of withholding reinforcement

Like punishment, withholding reinforcement is not very effective when used by itself, although it can be useful when combined with positive reinforcement. Here are four characteristics of withholding reinforcement that give you a more nuanced sense of how it works:

Gradual reduction in behavior. Although withholding reinforcement effectively decreases and often eliminates behavior, the process usually is very gradual, both initially and overall. It could take many days. Several unreinforced responses may occur before behavior begins to decline. When the undesirable behaviors are dangerous or severely disruptive, the delayed effects of withholding reinforcement can be unacceptable.

The burst. At the beginning of a program of withholding reinforcement, the frequency of the child's unwanted behavior may become greater than it was before the program began. Things really may get worse before they get better; that's the burst. Numerous examples of the burst pervade everyday experience. For example, turning on a radio (behavior) is usually followed by some sound (reinforcer). If the radio no longer works so that no reinforcement (sound) occurs, attempts to turn on the radio will eventually stop. However, before this occurs, the response may temporarily increase in frequency (several on/off turns) and in intensity or vigor. The same is likely to occur when you're trying to start your car. If the car won't start (the reinforcer is no longer forthcoming after turning the key — the behavior), you'll stop trying to start the car. But before you do stop, there's likely to be a rapid burst of several vigorous attempts to start the car.

In parenting, one place where you're likely to see the burst is in the going-to-bed ritual. Let's say that a child has a little tantrum and creates a scene before going to bed. The parents have been going into the room, reasoning and then shouting at the child—attention that could be maintaining the bedtime tantrums. The tantrums are not the parents' fault, but now that the tantrums are occurring, their attention could be the reinforcer maintaining the behavior. Say the parents read this book but skip the part about the burst, and they decide they're not going to attend to the tantrums anymore. That is, they're going to use withholding reinforcement. So on the first night the child goes to bed and has a tantrum, and the parents don't go into the room but just let it go. The tantrum lasts fifteen minutes before the child becomes quiet and apparently goes to sleep. So far, so good. On the second or perhaps third night, the parents are doing nothing different—still ignoring. But the child's tantrum goes to thirty minutes and is more intense, too—all worse than it was before the withholding reinforcement program started. The parents now say, "Hey, this withholding reinforcement business doesn't work." They may go into the room and provide attention and comfort or perhaps some reprimands. Such attention (parental reinforcement) will increase the probability of intense tantrums because it comes when the behavior is worse than usual, so from the child's point of view that's what's being reinforced: stepping up the tantrums to get attention. To the parents, of course, withholding reinforcement may appear to be failing because the behavior has become worse. However, the effects of the program are merely beginning; that is, the more intense tantrum means that it's working.

Parents, teachers, or other persons who may be involved in a withholding reinforcement program ought to be forewarned of the possibility of a burst so that they don't overreact to a temporary increase in the unwanted behavior. But my experience is that forewarning is not very helpful. In the midst of a burst and tantrum, the parents look at each other and say, "That psychologist knows nothing!" and desperately rush into the room to shout at the child, "You'd better get to sleep! Now stop fooling around, or we will take away your junior year in college once you get bigger."

Instead of or in addition to the forewarning, it's better to add positive reinforcement for positive opposites to the program, as I will explain in detail later. The combined program is much more likely to reduce the likelihood of the burst. All that said, an initial burst of responses does not always occur when withholding reinforcement is used on its own as the intervention. However, when it does occur, don't reinforce this more intense version of the unwanted behavior. The danger of falling into the trap of reinforcing that more intense behavior adds to the risk of relying on a withholding reinforcement program in the absence of other procedures.

Spontaneous recovery. So you have made it past the burst and apologized for those nasty things you said to your psychologist over the phone, and now the behavior (minutes of tantrum) may be declining. We are still not home free. After a program of withholding reinforcement has progressed, an unwanted behavior may temporarily reappear, even though it has not been reinforced. That's called *spontaneous recovery,* the temporary recurrence of a nonreinforced behavior. When a behavior comes back, it's usually not as bad (extreme, severe) as it was before the withholding reinforcement program started and not anywhere near as bad as the burst. For example, if a child's tantrums are ignored, the duration of tantrums will probably decrease over time, possibly after an initial burst of responses. Now let us say we are down to no tantrums on some nights and three or four minutes of light whimpering on other nights. Now out of the clear blue, there is spontaneous recovery in which one night the tantrum goes back up to ten minutes. This will probably drop out on the next night and the behavior will continue to decline.

But, as with the burst, a major concern raised by spontaneous recovery is that the response may be accidentally reinforced. When withholding reinforcement is proceeding well and then for no apparent reason the behavior increases rather than continues to decline, it's understandable that some parents will look at each other again and repeat, "Told you, that psychologist knows nothing!" and then run into the child's room and tell him to go to sleep or this time he will also lose his senior year of college. It's important to realize that the spontaneous recurrence of a response during a withholding reinforcement program doesn't necessarily reflect the ineffectiveness of the procedure. We don't know why this happens and can't predict when exactly it will happen, but we know it's a normal part of the process. You have to be disciplined and stick to your commitment to extinguish the behavior. Like the burst, the spontaneous recovery should pass quickly.

Possible side effects. Withdrawing reinforcement may result in the child having emotional responses such as agitation, frustration, rage, aggression, and feelings of failure. The transition from positive reinforcement to withholding reinforcement is aversive and leads to side effects similar to those evident with punishment. So, there are emotional effects, and sometimes aggression. This should be a familiar process. For example, what happens after you put money into a malfunctioning vending machine? Once it becomes clear that the machine won't reinforce your behavior with the usual soda or candy bar, you are likely to rage, curse, and physically attack it. When you're repeatedly trying to start your car (behavior) and the reinforcer (car starting) is not forthcoming (extinction), are you likely to be all smiles, or to shout and smack the steering wheel?

In other contexts, individuals who have experienced repeated reinforcement of certain responses respond to the cessation of such reinforcement as a failure. For example, when an athlete performs poorly, he may swear, consider himself a loser, and throw a tennis racket or baseball bat to the ground in disgust. The notion of a poor loser signifies a person who engages in emotional behavior when his or her responses are not reinforced in a contest—that is, when the crowd no longer roars approval and the pleasure of winning is denied. A silver lining: with a program of withholding reinforcement, when side effects occur, they are likely to be temporary and to diminish as the target response is extinguished. Consequently, the side effects are usually not as bad as those associated with punishment.

The key challenge: controlling
the source of reinforcement

Withholding reinforcement sounds easy enough, even if it's not very effective by itself. Identify the reinforcer after the behavior (often attention) and just stop giving it. Of course, it's not always that simple. First, you need to exercise very careful control over reinforcers. Any accidental reinforcement may rapidly bring back the behavior you are trying to get rid of and make the process of eliminating the behavior even longer. Second, there are many situations in which you can't easily control the reinforcer that follows the behavior. For example, reinforcement is particularly difficult to control when it's provided by siblings or peers. Playing with food at the dinner table among siblings or clowning in the classroom are examples where the other children are likely to be the main source of reinforcement. A common problem in schools is bullying, and among the many influences that maintain it are peer attention and peers joining in to abet the bully. In fact, as research on bullying shows, when peers do not provide supportive attention and actually try to intervene to stop the bullying, bullying usually stops within ten seconds.

It's virtually impossible to control reinforcement for some behaviors. Consider Willie Sutton, a famously colorful bank robber whose mastery of disguises became part of his renown. In his memoir he says, "Why did I rob banks? Because I enjoyed it. I loved it. I was more alive when I was inside a bank, robbing it, than at any other time in my life. I enjoyed everything about it so much that one or two weeks later I'd be out looking for the next job." For Willie, the more obvious reinforcers—free money, the submissiveness of people he robbed at gunpoint—actually didn't seem to matter very much. Many behaviors, including such confounding activities as self-harming (for example, cutting oneself) or head banging (among some children with autism), are reinforced by consequences associated with the behavior itself (reduction of anxiety, the stimulation and vibration of the hitting). You can see why identifying and controlling the reinforcer can be difficult. If we go back to the more common situation—attending to a behavior as the main reinforcer—even here it's not always easy to be consistent. Among the reasons is that a with-holding reinforcement program can take a long time, and you have to be diligent about not attending to the behavior as the gradual change occurs.

As a parent, you may make requests of your child to stop doing something, but the behavior is maintained by reinforcers not read-ily under your control. You may tell your child to stop bullying a sibling or neighbor, but bullying brings immediate reinforcement in the form of the victim's submission, and that connection is hard to control with delayed consequences. Or you would like your child to play computer games much less than he does, but that's hard to control because of the reinforcing value, the jolt of stimulation he gets when he plays the games. Parents of a fourteen-year-old boy came to the Yale Parenting Center because they had just dis-covered pornography on his computer in his room. The parents insisted that he stop watching and promised to take his computer away if they caught him disobeying. That approach was doomed to fail because of the rewarding value to the boy of searching for, finding, and watching the pornography. Sometimes the reinforcer can be identified, but extraordinary measures are needed to obtain control. In this example of Internet pornography, we helped the parents come up with a more promising plan: they tried to con-trol the behavior by moving the computer to the dining room and controlling their son's use of it so that he was never unsupervised while he was on it.

There are ways to change each of the behaviors just mentioned, and withholding reinforcement can play a role, but not the main role. For that we need positive reinforcement of positive opposites.

How to use withholding
reinforcement so it actually works

1. The single most important factor in using withholding re-inforcement is exactly the same as for punishment: it is a secondary procedure best used as a complement to a positive

reinforcement program. The effectiveness of withholding reinforcement depends on whether and how often the positive opposite is reinforced. Withholding reinforcement is a very slow process that often includes a return of the unwanted behavior in the form of the burst and spontaneous recovery. If one pairs withholding reinforcement with a strong reinforcement program, the undesired behavior drops out much more quickly and is less likely to come back in bursts along the way.

2. Be as sure as you can that the behavior you are trying to extinguish is not maintained by some reinforcer other than your attention. If your attention is not the reinforcer maintaining the behavior (as in the case of Danica's brothers thinking her food antics were funny), your ignoring the behavior will completely fail. Ask yourself, "When my child does this behavior, is there any response that occurs to maintain it?" If that's the case, make sure you end those consequences if you can. If you can't, withholding reinforcement won't work, but don't give up hope. Reinforcement of positive opposites should do the trick.

Dos

- Identify any consequences that might be following and helping maintain the behavior you want to eliminate.
- Try to break that connection so the consequence (often it's attention, and remember that even a reprimand can reinforce) is not provided anymore.
- Immediately consider what a positive opposite would be and start a reinforcement program for that.

Don'ts

- Don't believe that merely ceasing to provide attention will work very effectively. Withholding reinforcement is slow and not very effective when used alone.
- Don't accidentally reinforce the unwanted behavior. The burst and spontaneous recovery will put you to the test!

- Don't forget about positive reinforcement. Withholding reinforcement does not work very well when used by itself, but it
  can work very well when it's part of a program that also reinforces positive opposites.

Conclusion

Punishment and withholding reinforcement are consequences that
can have a role in changing behavior as part of our ABCs. They share
some important characteristics. First, by itself, neither punishment
nor withholding reinforcement is likely to be very effective. The reason is that neither teaches or develops the behavior you want. Neither offers opportunities for reinforced practice, so punishment and
withholding reinforcement must remain secondary procedures, part
of a larger program that centers on positively reinforcing the behavior one wishes.

Punishment and withholding reinforcement can be useful ad-
juncts. Mild punishment in the form of a look, gesture, statement,
brief time out, or brief loss of a privilege can be effective if a positive
reinforcement program is in place. Withholding reinforcement is important, too, because it's often useful to ask whether the disruptive
behavior might unwittingly be maintained by some reinforcer in the
setting. Attention (from siblings, peers, adults) is a likely culprit, or
the behavior itself (for example, fighting, shouting) may lead to its
own reinforcement (for example, submission by others). We want
to break connections between inappropriate behavior and unwit-
ting consequences that might maintain that behavior. Often that's
not easy to do. Happily, we do not have to break the connection to
change behavior. Reinforcement of positive opposites can still help
here. Even so, always check what could be maintaining that disruptive behavior and try to stop those consequences if feasible.

5

The Routines of Family Life
Creating the Context for Success

So far we've focused on filling your parenting kit with tools that can be used to alter specific behaviors and develop broader characteristics like cooperation, persistence, or generosity. But this chapter takes a step back from the nuts-and-bolts details of the ABCs to consider broader issues of parenting, the context or background of daily life. Psychologists call this context a "nurturing environment," and they devote effort to studying it because it makes a huge difference in how your child functions. The quality of a nurturing environment also directly affects your use of the ABCs, the tools in the toolkit, because it can have a strong effect on whether and how challenges emerge in your child's behavior, and on the ease or difficulty you encounter in addressing them.

A nurturing environment is to the psychological development of a child like exercise and physical activity are to her physical well-being. Exercise and activity—running around, playground visits, playing games outside, walking instead of going everywhere by car—are good for the body in the short and long run. They are a background set of activities that have broad effects on health, including decreasing the likelihood that a wide range of mental and physical problems will occur later in your child's life. Exercise in this general sense is not a specific treatment for some problem—as opposed to, say, particular leg-strengthening exercises used to treat a knee injury. Similarly, as parents you can create a nurturing environment in the home that can influence the general health and functioning of your child and make child rearing less challenging.

Providing a nurturing environment is discussed less in the media than exercise, but both are very well studied scientifically. And the bodies of research on both show that a nurturing environment and exercising share similarities in their benefits. Both are related to

- Mental health—better adjustment, fewer negative symptoms such as depression, greater ability to manage and reduce anxiety and stress
- Physical health—stronger immune system, less illness, a longer life span more likely
- Academic functioning—better performance in school, greater chance of graduating high school or college

Providing a nurturing home environment doesn't replace the tools I have described, and the tools don't substitute for a nurturing environment. Rather, they work together to bring out the best in your child and to put him on the best course that you as a parent can provide. Most children's lives eventually happen out of the home; the context you create for their lives in the home provides a sound preparation for that.

In this chapter I'll address several different aspects of providing a nurturing environment. They're all science-tested and valuable, and I urge you as you read to consider each in turn—even those that might already seem familiar to you—and how it might fit into your life. It may be difficult for you to imagine doing all of them all the time, but don't panic. Think about other recommendations you've seen that are based on sound research. Recommendations for how to eat in a healthy way, for instance, now often depend on the idea of a food plate as a guide. The plate has various portions of what we ought to eat as part of a healthy diet to control weight, slow aging, and reduce our risk for many diseases. Probably nobody can meet every single guideline and eat the recommended amounts of nuts, fruits, beans, whole grains, vegetables, and so on in a given day, but any effort you can make in that direction will help. It's worthwhile to do your level best to incorporate as many of these recommendations as you can into your habits.

As you read this chapter's survey of ways to foster a nurturing environment, think of it as a kind of psychological food plate for parenting and family life. I realize that it's unlikely that anyone can implement every recommendation on any given day, but your family will benefit from whatever part of it you can do. It's not an all-or-nothing proposition; try to do as much as you reasonably can. And, in addition to describing a number of basic features of family life that parents may be able to control for the good of the family, I'm also going to add a sort of No-No Plate of things you should limit or eliminate from your household, to the extent possible.

1. Promote good communication with your child as early as possible

Good communication refers to genuine exchanges in which you and your child talk to each other and, even more important, listen to each other. The specific topics under discussion matter less than developing and sustaining open lines of communication. Your child needs someone to help cope with and handle the stressors of her life, a person to turn to for sympathetic attention and advice as childhood blooms into adolescence. Anything you can do to enable communication is a significant investment in your child's well-being.

Most parents feel and say that their children can talk to them about anything. In principle and at some high level of abstraction they are absolutely right. Yet, while most children *want* to go to their parents about difficult topics, they often shy away from actually doing it because they expect that when they raise the touchy subject, the parent will respond with an opinion, directive, family ethical imperative ("We *never* . . ."), or dated story only vaguely related to the child's concerns. All of these typical parental reactions are aversive, leading to avoidance (as I described in chapter four) of even discussing such topics.

It's common for us as parents to feel that we have shown such deep and consistent commitment—think endless diapers, cleanups, sitting up with our sick child—that our children must know we're there for them. They do, in fact, know that, but knowing it is not the same as actually coming to you to talk about a difficult topic. The latter is a behavior, and, as I've explained earlier, when it comes to behavior, knowing and doing are pretty much unrelated. But if your child can come to you to discuss difficult situations with some confidence, based on experience, that you will listen and not preach or rant, this will greatly help his adjustment to stressors and traumas in everyday life. Also, open lines of communication will help you identify problems in their early stages and intervene long before they escalate. What makes this all especially interesting is that children actually prefer to talk to their parents about difficult topics—sex, drugs, you name it—rather than to their peers. So it pays to reduce the barriers that prevent them from doing so.

What you can do
First, get rid of saying to your child, or say no more than once per year, "You can talk to me about anything." Such a general reassurance about your approachability is what we call an "oblique antecedent," indirect and very far away from the behavior it encourages (it may be months before something comes up that the child feels he has to discuss with you) and is not likely to influence your child actually to come to you. Also, the proof is in what you model, not what you say. Ask yourself if it's really true that your child can come to you to talk about anything. Is the gate truly open, or, at least when it comes to certain touchy topics, does your child feel that there is actually a twelve-foot-thick wall she couldn't even try to blast through?

Second, listen to your child and her opinions, not only because it's good for her mental health and self-esteem but because of the exchange it represents. You listen because you want your child to share her views with you, and you expect the same level of attention from her. Think of negotiation not just as you talking and then your child talking but as you listening and then your child listening. That's the key. Your modeling of this behavior early in life will make later interactions with your child much easier. How do you know if you are really listening? Well, if you're waiting for your child to stop talking so you can correct her misconceptions, that's a pretty good definition of not listening. If you're thinking that something in what your child is saying might be new, deeply felt, and possibly disturbing, and that you need to respond by acknowledging that it's important, asking for clarification, or encouraging your child to give you more details about his experience, those are pretty good signs that you're listening.

Third and related, be an "askable" parent. This term is used to describe parents whose children feel comfortable coming to them to talk, especially about touchier subjects like intimacy, relationships, sexual orientation, substance use, confessions—in other words, about life. One key to being askable is how you respond during the conversation. After you've heard what your child has to say, do not begin by refuting it. Point out anything good in what your child said and praise your child for coming to you about it at all, to reinforce openness and exchange, even if you then propose a different way of thinking about it. And never use *dumb, stupid,* or other belittling words.

"Of course," you're thinking. "What kind of idiot would do that?" Well, lots of parents, even good and loving parents, do something like it. Again, and be honest with yourself: when your child talks, does he get the feeling that you're just impatiently waiting for him to finish so that you can state your opinion at length and in detail?

As an early teen, one of my daughters figured out how to get me to talk with her about an important topic that might ordinarily lead to my predictable judgmental reactions. Once in a while she would ask if we could talk "as friends" rather than father and daughter. A normal reaction would be for me to riff on how dads and friends are different, how I am not her friend in some ways and better than a friend in other ways, how *dad* spelled backwards is still *dad* but *friend* makes no sense when spelled backwards, and so on. But because she caught me off guard the first time, before I'd had a chance to rehearse my "not-friend" speech, I had no real choice but to agree. Asking me to talk as friends was a setting event, an effective antecedent that made me less likely to fall back on the usual parental judgments. (She had intuited a lesson from this book's first chapter, that getting behavior you want is as much about antecedents as about consequences.)

After all, when friends speak to each other about important or intimate topics, they don't usually hammer each other with statements like "That was terrible judgment! How many times have I told you not to do that?" My daughter wanted to talk with me about some relationship problem she was having—nothing shocking, but it mattered to her. She just wanted to lay it out and tell me what she thought, and she wanted me to listen nonjudgmentally and not weigh in with a solution. This was one of several requests she made during her teen years to suspend our usual roles for a moment in order to communicate better and differently. And I tried to let her modeling of this approach influence me; as she got a little older, I tried to tell her stories about my own experiences that would be of interest but did not have a moralizing message.

That brings up one more thing you can do: be a model for your child by talking about your own daily life. I don't mean baring your soul in an uncomfortable way ("I never truly loved your mother") or stressing your child with complaints or gossip about family or work ("I'm telling you, my supervisor is a total drunken SOB"). Rather, I mean that you can model talking about your life—stories about your own school days, stories about your workday, stories about minor frustrations and small pleasures and vivid memories. Modeling exchanges of this sort will do more to make you an askable parent than will declaring to your child, "You can talk to me about anything."

2. Build positive family connections

Promoting good communication between you and your child early will certainly be a plus to family life, but the parent-child bond and communication are part of a larger family network that's also important. Whether you've got a big family in your home or just a single parent and a child, the quality of interactions with relatives living in the home and beyond it can be of great help in promoting positive behavior by your child. Children with positive family lives do better in school and are less likely to show behavioral problems and symptoms of clinical dysfunction. That family life makes such a difference can hardly be news. But what you can do and its impact may come as news to you.

What you can do
First, the quality of family life is greatly influenced by rituals and routines that give structure to the week, the month, the year. The research suggests that the regularity of the activities is what's important, rather than the specific content of them. Having such rituals and routines helps reduce stress and anxiety among children and helps them avoid some risky behaviors as they turn into teens and young adults.

Rituals and routines can be extremely modest. Every Friday afternoon you might go food shopping, for instance, or on Saturdays you have a pancake breakfast, or you stop at a certain park when you come home from Grandma's house, and so on. A regular drive to ballet or swimming can double as both simple logistics and a week-ordering routine that gives you a regular time to talk about how things are going with friends, school, romance, and so on. Aim for regularity and frequency, but don't be so rigid that the routine becomes an additional source of pressure. You're trying here to build a reservoir of predictable experiences—which, in addition to all the other benefits, will become the basis of good memories. Good experiences founded in routines will build your relationship and make you more effective in everything you do as a parent, whether you are focusing on the usual ABCs with a younger child or on potentially serious issues with an older one. Small regular investments in your relationship are like regular deposits in your savings account. They accrue slowly, and the added amount at any given moment may look like nothing, but the compound interest, building on what was added before, is enormous.

Second, connect your child to other family members, including

those of different generations. There are lots of benefits of such connections, including family routines that stabilize a child's life, and
opportunities for the child to bond with and learn from adults who
aren't his parents, a skill he's going to need to develop in life. Ex-
tended-family connections have not been widely studied in relation
to children's behavior, but some recent research shows that children
with connections to extended family have a reduced risk of problem
behaviors.

Families tend to spread out, so it's not always easy to keep in
touch, but try to build relationships that provide for continuity and
roots with older generations but also for bonding with any of your
child's closer-in-age relatives—cousins, for instance. If they live far
away, it's worth bringing everyone together during the holidays, even
if all parties have to travel to meet in the middle. If you're not around
extended family, and especially if you're a single parent, perhaps try
to make some time—a picnic or outing, say, or any kind of visit—in
which you and your child can spend time with another single parent
with a child. Often a church or other community connection is a
good way to find such peers, and there's at least one international or-
ganization for single parents and their children. Also, you can establish routines for using social networking (Skype, Facebook) to keep
in touch with a grandmother, uncle, or cousin.

Finally, don't buy into the myth of quality time; value quantity
time, and provide as much of it as your life allows. Be around, be
together, and maintain family routines linked to regular household
business, like meals and errands. This kind of mundane quantity time
is much more significant than that one memorable quality-time outing to a big event at which you spend a lot of money. Quality time
is nice, but it's never a substitute for quantity time. Imagining that it
might be was the rationale of a busy generation. A very special forty
minutes of parent-and-child time per weekend is a good thing—and
it's lovely if you don't spend that time arguing—but you need plenty
of quantity time as well to help get the child to the place you might
like him to be in life.

Think about quantity versus quality in reading to your child.
It's better to read pretty good children's stories to her every day for

twenty minutes than to go all week without reading to her and then on Sunday read the greatest children's book of all time to her for three hours. She's going to get a lot more out of a daily dose of reading, and it's far more likely to positively affect her reading skills and academic performance.

One appealing thing about quantity time is that you don't have to do anything special or have a scheduled activity; just arrange to be together, to be available to each other and interact normally.

3. Promote positive social behavior

Positive social behavior is a broad term covering the ability to interact with others in constructive ways. I'm talking here about the basics of getting along with others: cooperating, being sensitive or responsive to others, maintaining relationships, being able to engage with others. These behaviors vary markedly over the course of one's life as different types of relationships emerge, a sequence that begins with a child's relationship to parents and siblings and extends to playmates, friends, schoolmates, teachers, eventually a spouse or partner, and, in time, perhaps your child's own children. In childhood, the basis of such relationships throughout life takes form.

We know that children who engage in positive social behaviors do better in their schoolwork and also are less likely to engage in disruptive behavior, bullying, and substance use and abuse. Over the years, research has shown that these positive social behaviors are especially important early in life. To prepare children for entering school, for many years the emphasis was on giving them early exposure to academic activities, such as learning how to read as early as possible. To be sure, such activities are important, but current views focus more on social behavior, preparing children for school by developing their ability to interact with others, to cooperate, share, play nicely, and listen to adults. This is understandable. No child gets kicked out of daycare or even first grade for failing to master multiplication tables or the interpretation of *Curious George,* but children, including three-year-olds in daycare, do get suspended all the time for failures in social behavior—the negative opposite of those basic social skills I just mentioned. So positive social behaviors are important early in life, and their importance continues in the elementary through high school years, and of course into and throughout adulthood.

Some children come into the world ready to be in a receiving line, to smile, greet, and welcome every stranger on the planet. But most of us are not in that group, so it's good to know that there are ways to help our children develop positive social behaviors. We know all this from studies that actually develop social behavior and evaluate its benefits over time and across many areas of functioning. At the Yale Parenting Center, we have studied this for decades and have shown that when positive social behaviors are developed in children who are having difficulties, many other parts of their lives change, including improved school functioning, better peer relations at school, better family relations, and fewer symptoms of psychiatric disorders.

What you can do
Help your child develop good relations with others as opportunities arise, and, with reinforced practice in mind, look for ways to increase the number of opportunities for positive social behaviors, especially if they're not occurring often enough now to reinforce and build on. Children come into the world with different temperaments; there are biological propensities for being withdrawn, shy, flexible, gregarious, extroverted, and all shades in between. Any parent with one child understands this, but parents with two or more children are often stunned by how two children can be so different so early in life. Differences in temperament mean that different children will find it more or less natural or easy to do certain things, like being social.

If social relations come pretty easily to your child, it won't take much work for you to cultivate these skills. A play date, a sleepover, taking one of her friends with you on a family outing once in a while—that might be all that's needed. Also, if there are neighbors to play with casually or other play opportunities that require little arrangement, all the better. As your child engages in social interaction, monitor how he is doing. Especially with younger children, parents almost always monitor for safety, but I'm talking about a different kind of attention to your child at play. Do you see any problems with sharing, taking turns, being reasonable with the other person? If you're seeing a repeated negative social behavior that you want to address, go immediately to the next and all-important step: What are the positive opposites for you to develop?

The strategies outlined in prior chapters might be helpful if a particular area needs a little work. That is, think about antecedents to help promote a particular social behavior, shape to develop small activities that may help along the way, and use special praise for the right kind of interactions. You may need to help out a lot, especially in the early stages—for instance, by walking a younger child to the park and staying nearby (setting events to make it easier for positive social behavior to occur). Commands ("Just go over there and play with those kids like everyone else") are not very useful as prompts for many children. Better to accompany the child and look for slight social behavior to reinforce, like playing near someone or handing another child a toy. Let your child be your guide as to where shaping begins. Remember, when it comes to a particular aptitude or behavior, shaping begins with just a slight step up from what your child actually does now.

Even if your child is withdrawn and doesn't start up with others easily, you can still work on social relations. Start with small doses, not a full sleepover or four-hour play date. Shaping and a more gradual approach can really help. If that still seems like a stretch for your child, have him select a friend to accompany all of you on a family outing to the beach, an amusement park, whatever you enjoy. Your child and his friend will be together, but your child has the security of your presence as you begin the process of shaping that will eventually lead to more independent socialization without you so close by.

You can do plenty to help your child build social skills, and your efforts will pay off. As your child reaches school age and leaves the home more and more on her own, her adjustment will be much better if she is socially adept. That doesn't mean she has to be popular; research shows the benefits and protections of social support can stem from having even just one friend.

Another way to help build positive social relations is to develop one or more competencies in a child that involve or eventually will involve activities with other people. It's useful to help your child develop some skill, interest, or talent that can continue over many years and pay dividends in social engagement. In relation to social behavior, not all areas are equal. That is, some are more likely to promote interactions and connections with other people over time. So first-person-shooter video games don't hold much promise, but music lessons, for instance, not only build skill on an instrument, but they also bring the child into contact with other children at lessons, recitals, school orchestras, and perhaps loud jam sessions in your home. Music entails many solo hours of practice, of course, but they lead to engagement with others. Other arts (for example, theater, dance) and sports (such as gymnastics or baseball) may do the same in terms of building competence and fostering social behavior along the way.

You and your child will naturally select an activity according to your own preferences, but among the possible choices give special consideration to those activities that are likely to be more social over time and that are likely to be lifelong or nearly so. We want the child to be involved with others and to gain the mental and physical health benefits that socialization provides. We are talking about childhood, but the mental and physical benefits of positive social behaviors are lifelong.

4. Foster flexibility in your household

Flexibility refers to openness to change and compromise — and I'm talking about your own flexibility more than your child's. Flexibility can be difficult to accomplish when running a home because there's so much that cannot be flexible, such as getting out the door on time in the morning, ensuring that meals are on time, scheduling baby-sitting coverage, making sure that homework goes from the child's backpack to her desk to done and back into the backpack, and so on. In many contexts, *flexible* just sounds like another word for *loose,* and in many cases loose won't do.

But by "flexible" I mean trying to compromise when you can, and more and more as your child gets older and starts expressing preferences. The other extreme would be very clear and rigid statements delivered from authority: "Do it because I said so." You know now from your mastery of antecedents that such statements actually foster oppositional behavior and more noncompliance. And you also know that choice, real or in appearance, fosters compliance. In chapter one those lessons were related to specific strategies to change behavior, and here I bring up flexibility as a broader contextual influence, but the two kinds of flexibility are definitely related.

Flexibility and compromise represent a Goldilocks mean, a sweet spot, of parenting. It's difficult to be "just right." For example, we know that a child will have more behavior problems at home and at school when a parent is either too permissive (and is fairly unstructured and lays down few limits or guidelines) or too tight and restrictive (is authoritarian, controlling, with lots of rules and limits). Both extremes increase the risk for a negative outcome.

What you can do
There is much you can do to be flexible and set that as a tone for your family. You do need to set up consistent expectations for responsibilities at home and at school, and there's nothing wrong with maintaining high standards, but it's also useful to go out of your way to have discussions in which you listen to your child's view and make some decisions based on that.

Parents are often devoted to slippery-slope logic: "If I let this seemingly small thing go, I lose control, and my child will become a barbarian and will loot and burn our household, leaving no stone atop another." But that's typically the opposite of what happens. Go to war over every minor thing and you will lose both the battles and the war. You will also do some harm to your long-term relationship with your child, by making her more likely to see you as an unapproachable rather than an askable parent. And the metaphor of battles and war is misguided from the outset because it suggests that you are pitted against your child. A better metaphor: You are sailing a ship toward a goal of a well-adjusted, functioning, non-freeloading adulthood for your child. This requires tacking, which can look as if one is veering away from the goal, but tacking is often the best way to take advantage of the prevailing wind and make progress toward the goal.

Compromise when you can, and let some things go when you can. Consider bedtime, curfew, messy room, and weird personal appearance as areas in which you can give a little. When you give a little there, you can gain credibility, control, and reasonableness when the topics shift to rings through unlikely orifices, taking two years off high school to learn about the retro hippie network in the Southwest, and other subjects more likely to inspire a categorical *No!* from you.

At the Yale Parenting Center we find it helpful to discuss with parents whether they can bend or give in on some of their specific concerns. Parents and families differ, and it's important to find the flexible areas in each case. These areas of "give" can be little things for young children—loosening the rules around foods to eat on a given night, or what to wear on a given day—but for teens the process of negotiating can be more daunting and the stakes go up. One thing we suggest to parents is that they be less concerned about stage- or age-related events that are not likely to be harmful in themselves, are not likely to have permanent effects, and are part of the teen's age or culture. So torn jeans, orange hair, even a small nose stud—all stage-related, and maybe you can let them go. Or maybe not; each family is different, as I said, and flexibility differs in each case. But there are other situations—very provocative clothing, dating older men, using birth control at ages eleven and twelve (all issues that have come up at the Parenting Center)—that take the stakes up several notches and can lead in many directions to effects that last well beyond any temporary stage of development. In these cases you would be on sound ground not to compromise. When you're dealing with a matter somewhere in the middle—what time your child comes home from school, when and how often he checks in with you when he's out, using the computer, buying music files—can you reach an agreement that considers your child's views? Remember, if you're thinking slippery slope as the rationale for not wavering, you are likely to make yourself less effective as a parent and less likely to be a resource as someone to come to in time of need.

Flexibility and compromise are not primarily about the specific detail you may be negotiating. They're about your broader parenting style. In these negotiations you're also promoting positive communication, establishing yourself as askable, and modeling reasonableness.

5. Monitor the child and limit opportunities for behavioral problems

Monitoring means keeping track of where your child is, what he's doing, and whom he's with. Monitoring is most important for physical safety in the early years. Obviously, you don't want your toddler running into the street, getting onto playground equipment in ways that she's not ready for, or going off with strangers. But monitoring also plays a very large role in your child's adjustment, particularly in the preteen and teen years, and is an important contextual influence on development.

Whether children are monitored relates directly to the behavioral problems they experience. The teenage children of parents who monitor their whereabouts and activities are much less likely to engage in sexual activity and illicit drug use and other risky behavior. Also, more intense monitoring is associated with greater reduction in risk taking. This is referred to as a "dose-response relation": the higher the dose, the greater the impact. If you feel awkward and uncool about hounding your poor child, remember that there's a strong dose-response relation between monitoring and decreased risk. It's important to mention that risky behavior has important implications for physical health; we're still talking about basic safety, in a sense. Sexual activity in the young is usually unprotected, and the risk of sexually transmitted disease is a concern. Illicit drug use relates to overdose, more risky behavior, and death and serious injury, often car-related. All of this is documented, not merely scare tactics.

I want to make clear that monitoring is very compatible with giving your child freedom and responsibility. It doesn't mean keeping her at home, or driving her everywhere, or fearing the world. The witch knew where Rapunzel was—up in the tower, locked away from the world—but that didn't make her a model parent (and, by the way, it turns out that the witch didn't know who Rapunzel was spending time with in the tower, or what they were doing, a good illustration of the truth that lockdown isn't the same as monitoring). Knowing where your child is, who else is there, and who's in charge should go hand in hand with equipping and encouraging her self-confidently to explore her world, a goal incompatible with hovering-helicopter surveillance, obsessive check-ins every few minutes, and setting fearful, drastic limits on your child's movements.

One area where monitoring frequently comes up is after-school time, which can be difficult to keep track of if both parents are at work. It's even more difficult for a single parent. Yet you do need to know where your child is after school, whom he's with, and what he's doing. Not only are adolescents who are not monitored generally more likely to engage in all sorts of risky behavior, but lack of supervision after school is specifically associated with greater depression and poor grades.

In general, over the course of development, boys engage in more risky behavior than do girls. There can be many reasons for this, but one of them is thought to be the fact that parents monitor teenage girls more closely than they do boys. For example, girls have earlier curfews and more household chores to do. There's nothing fair or enlightened about this gender difference, but it has the effect of reducing girls' risk taking and improving their outcomes.

But there is more to monitoring than coplike surveillance, and quality matters as much as quantity. The members of families in which parents monitor their children have stronger ties, are more involved with one another, have warmer relationships, and are more cohesive and communicate better. A more approachable, askable parent with a warm relationship to a child will have more success in monitoring without turning into a warden. To that end, it helps to make monitoring normal and mutual in your household, which you can model by talking to your children about your day at the dinner table or during rides in the car. It also helps to begin early. Monitoring will not work if all of a sudden when your child hits age twelve you develop a new intense interest in her whereabouts that takes the form of verbal waterboarding. Also, making your home a place where your child can bring friends while you are there is a form of low-key monitoring that strikes a compromise with the adolescent brain's craving for contact with peers.

In the twenty-first century, monitoring your child's whereabouts to limit opportunities for problem behaviors is a commitment that extends into the virtual world. First, you have to set limits on access to computers, smartphones, tablets, and other such devices. Here, too, if you can't monitor how the computer is being used, all sorts of untoward things can happen: children and adolescents can readily get to sites that you would not approve of (pornography sites, for instance), engage in activities that can promote problem behaviors (video games and activities that focus on violence, stealing, and general hatefulness), and get caught up in online bullying.

What you can do

Establish early in the child's life that all family members routinely should know where everyone is. As your child is developing, make it natural to ask about activities at the dinner table. Make sure to establish a routine of monitoring and caring about where other family members are. The objective here is not a family police state; rather, it's a household in which everyone takes a supportive interest in the lives and well-being of others. Establishing that climate will save you, years later, from the chore of ineffectively interrogating your teen to determine where he was and what he was doing during the fifty-three extra minutes it took him to get home from school.

For older children and teens, you might try to develop the habit of calling in periodically (not every minute) to keep in touch. The cell phone has had plenty of bad effects on family life—distraction, separation, bad manners, and so on—but it does have the virtue of providing a handy way for older children to keep in touch.

Limiting the child's opportunity for problem behavior involves knowing whom she's with. Let's say your child is going to a friend's house after school. That sounds good and maybe especially good because you are fostering social relations, which we have already covered. But it could also be unwise. Will there be an adult at the house? Is that adult responsible or flaky? Perhaps give the parents over there a call before the event to confirm. Your child might say, "What, you don't trust me?" It's a fair question. The answer is yes, but your child is still a child, which means you need to know what's going on. We know already from piles of studies that the teenage years are a time when risky behavior increases; that's common. We know too that when teens are with each other and no adults are directly involved, risky behavior goes up a notch.

You are trying to get your child through a difficult period. That doesn't mean you'll cut out all risk—or would want to cut it all out, since adolescents who take no risks at all tend toward the same negative life outcomes (greater risk for poor physical and mental health in adulthood) as those who take too many—but it does mean that you want to channel that risk-taking impulse away from danger, especially by minimizing situations in which such dangerous risk taking is more likely to take place.

Another thing you can do is to build and model bonds to conventional values; working hard in school, time with family, and constructive extracurricular activities are still rewarded in the long run in our society. Developing these values early in childhood reduces the likelihood of aggressive behavior and risky activities later during adolescence, for instance. I have seen many parents loudly dismiss the value of classes their children are attending or comment freely on the incompetence of a specific teacher or schoolteachers in general. Yes, they're modeling candor, but at the price of undermining values that in the long run will greatly increase the likelihood of their child making it to adulthood ready for the next phases of life. (If it helps, remember that your child probably did not select his school; you probably did.)

Establishing routines and rituals within the family—special holidays, meals, weekly errands done together with a child, activities in the home that are a regular part of everyday life—can facilitate bonding to the family. Your evident valuing of reading and learning, of teachers and their mission, of doing well in school, and of other aspects of education will be helpful in a preventive way later. This doesn't mean expecting perfect or even necessarily high achievement, but it does mean explicitly valuing academic effort and an appreciation of school. And it also obliges you to model the behavior you want: not only respect for school but also moderation, reason, hard work, whatever you expect of your children. The research shows, for instance, that parents who talk about the riskiness of substance abuse and who don't engage in it themselves measurably reduce their children's risk.

6. Minimize negative social and psychological conditions for the child

I have been talking about making the most of positive contextual influences that will make child rearing a little easier and that will boost the likelihood that your child can function well in different ways: physical and mental health, school performance, relations with other people, and more. These contextual influences also increase the effectiveness of all of the strategies I have discussed in the other chapters. When the nurturing environment is strong, everything works better: antecedents, shaping, praise, even (brief, mild) punishment.

But then there's the other side: trying to minimize conditions that are harmful to development. Several household conditions can be toxic in the sense that they have negative short- and long-term effects on child development. At the extreme, I don't think I need to tell you that physical abuse of any kind puts a child at risk for a variety of serious negative outcomes and can greatly harm physical and mental health, but less extreme household conditions can also have very negative effects, and here I think I can pass along some advice derived from the research that may be of use to you.

Children living in stressful environments because of their interactions with others can suffer surprising negative effects. For instance, changes that have been identified in the brains of children under prolonged stress in the home appear to underlie not only the psychological symptoms you'd expect, such as depression and anxiety, but also deficits in verbal IQ. Even when a child isn't being physically abused, the damage is biological. For example, if a child is subjected to verbal or emotional abuse by parents on a regular basis or continually exposed to parental conflict in the home, the range of undesirable outcomes includes a weakening of the child's immune system, so that he's more likely to get sick. If the stress conditions continue—and we don't know exactly how long they must continue to have this effect—the weakening of the immune system endures and his system doesn't bounce back. This is why children who grow up in harsh and stressful environments do not live as long as they otherwise would be expected to and are more likely eventually to die of cancer, heart disease, and other serious diseases. And verbal abuse is only one producer of consistent stress. Others include a parent turning hot and cold emotionally or being wildly inconsistent in rules and enforcement, so that the child can't depend on her.

I talked about building routines and rituals and how important they are. The other side of that coin, a household without enough routines, falls into a state sometimes called "family chaos." Its main trait is not enough predictability in parents' behavior and family activities. It puts a lot of stress on a child when she doesn't know if or when dinner will happen on a given night, or whether she can count on her parents for a ride, when bedtime will be, or whether the rules have changed and how strictly they will be enforced. One father we saw at the Yale Parenting Center generally didn't care about chores but, when he'd had too much to drink, screamed at his child for not doing all of the dishes, and he pulled him out of bed at night to "finish the job" in the kitchen. The exact standard isn't what's important here; each home can set its own. But big swings in standards or in what's likely to happen when a standard isn't met can become a major stressor. Routines and rituals allay a child's anxiety and make for a much more harmonious home life; chaos in routines and wide fluctuations in parents' behavior increase the child's risk for many problems related to stress, anxiety, and behavior problems in school.

A word on punishment, specifically corporal punishment. Regular hitting of a child, even if it doesn't reach the legal definition of child abuse (which usually means leaving marks on the child and/or using an object other than one's hand to hit), can have exactly the effects we are talking about on physical well-being (depressing the function of the immune system), psychological well-being (increasing aggressive behavior, for example), and academic functioning (making strong academic achievement less likely and placement in special classes for behavioral problems more likely).

There is no reason to panic because you argue with your spouse or yell at your children now and then or have even swatted your child on a rare occasion. Most people with spouses or children do that. We're talking about sustained, ongoing stress, not the usual ups and downs of family life.

Among the challenges for us as parents is that often we do not know the sources of the child's stress. For example, bullying is one of the most stressful experiences schoolchildren report, and their parents usually are unaware of it. The challenge of helping with children's stressors increases because children experience their own stress but also the spillover of their parents' stress. Parental stress, whether it's caused by financial problems or difficulties at work or relationship woes, filters down to the child.

What you can do
Stress is part of normal life. You can start by making sure that your child isn't getting an overdose of it in the form of prolonged household conflict, relentless belittling and dismissive comments, harsh and frequent punishment, or unreasonable levels of family chaos.

In any life there will be crises, such as divorce, moving the child away from friends and a familiar school, bouncing back and forth in joint custody, and the like. These can be very stressful. Try to be as comforting and understanding as possible, and to keep activities and routines as consistent as possible with pre-crisis activities (especially if the crisis is a divorce). One of the lessons that authorities and researchers have learned from responses to natural disasters like hurricanes, earthquakes, and tsunamis is that they need to be ready in advance to get the schools open again as fast as possible after the disaster hits. Among the many positive effects of a return to school is the sense of returning families to a familiar routine and sense of purpose.

The specific tools and strategies I've outlined in the previous chapters can have a positive influence on the overall conditions of stress that are toxic to a child. Our own studies at Yale have shown that parents who carry out the strategies we teach (ABCs) to change a child's behavior are more consistent in their parenting, which lowers the stress on all members of the household. Not only does the child's behavior improve, but parents who are no longer winging it in angry desperation experience much less stress in their lives. That lowers the stress on both parents and children in a mutually reinforcing way, and family relationships improve.

This is a good place to make an important point about the mutually supporting relationship between the contextual influences I'm talking about in this chapter and the tools and skills (the ABCs) I've presented to you in the chapters that came before. When you use the ABCs, you not only change your child's behavior, you also change your household's psychological climate, the context. And the reverse is also true: when you work to improve the context, one major benefit is that it makes your use of the ABCs to change behavior more effective. Improving context by improving communication with your child or strengthening her bond to constructive values won't, all by itself, get her to complete her homework or not beat up her brother, but it makes it easier for you to use the ABCs successfully to address specific matters like homework or fighting.

Finally, in terms of what you can do, I have been emphasizing praise as a way to change behavior. The praise I've covered in this book is very strategic (you want to change something in the child) and has to be done in a special way to be effective (enthusiastic, state exactly what you are praising, end with a nonverbal pat, touch, high-five). In terms of stressors and helping your child, the other, not-so-strategic kind of praise and affection is also important. Hugs, expressions of love and support, and clear indications of the joy you take in your child all are important to build the secure attachment of your child to you. That secure attachment will improve your child's development and also provide a foundation to address the often daunting challenges of life once the child begins leaving the home. When we ask parents who come to the Yale Parenting Center if they praise their children, they invariably say yes, a lot, all the time. They're talking about the general nonstrategic praise that makes for a great context for a developing child. We end up focusing with them on strategic praise, as part of the ABCs to change child behavior, the kind of praise that virtually no parent does without special training (or reading this book). Both types are important, and one does not substitute for the other.

7. Minimize negative biological conditions

We know more and more about the intricate relationship between physical and psychological health. I've just gone over some ways in which psychological influences or experiences such as being stressed or feeling ostracized can affect physical health—by, for example, weakening the immune system. Also, we know that the reverse influence also occurs: research on adults shows, for example, that physiological or biological conditions such as a heart attack or taking medications for various disorders can influence psychological health—affecting the onset of depression or disturbances in thinking.

But biological factors that influence your child's psychological health are less well understood than many online sources would have us believe. On the Web, for example, there's unlimited advice about special diets and which foods to consume or avoid, and you will find assurances that various vitamins and hormones, spices, or suppositories will prevent and treat all sorts of conditions related to child development, especially psychological disorders like attention deficit hyperactivity disorder, autism, or depression. Most of the claims turned up by a Google search are just not supported by research. It is so difficult for us as citizens to tell what is promising and might be helpful and what is just an opinion with no strong basis. The difference is important because many ineffective elixirs stop people from seeking more effective interventions. Also, some have harmful side effects.

Yet we do know that some biological factors do promote or thwart child development, and we can highlight main influences. First, prenatal habits and nutrition are important beyond the obvious physical development of the child. Substance use in pregnancy such as cigarette smoking and moderate to heavy alcohol use is well known to relate to various physical conditions that can afflict a child (for example, defects in the heart and kidneys, facial abnormalities), but it also relates to behavioral and psychological problems such as hyperactivity, aggression, and learning disabilities. The relations are not one to one in the sense that all early exposures of the fetus to these substances invariably lead to these other outcomes. But substance use, along with poor diet during pregnancy and general poor health of the mother, increase the risk (that is, the likelihood) of behavioral problems emerging in the child. Yet it's also true, and this is an especially frustrating aspect of these relationships, that a parent can engage in the very best prenatal habits and things can still go wrong in the child's development.

A few toxins in the environment that can influence a child's behavior are known and ought to be controlled. Cigarette smoke is a primary example. Children who have secondary exposure to cigarette smoke in the home—that is, the children don't smoke, but their parents or others in the house do—are much more likely to have behavioral problems, including aggressive and hyperactive behaviors, as well as a variety of respiratory diseases, hay fever, ear diseases, eczema, heart disease, sudden infant death syndrome, cognitive deficits (impairment of thought processes), reduced math and reading skills, and premature death.

Are the behavior problems caused by the cigarette smoke and its residues? We aren't certain yet, but many other potential contributing factors have been isolated and evaluated, including parents' income and education levels, which are also related to child health, and they don't explain away the correlation between cigarette smoke and children's behavior problems. Again, we can't conclude that the smoke causes behavioral problems in all children, but it does make such problems more likely. National surveys in the United States as well as many other studies have shown that children in homes where at least one parent smokes are much more likely to show aggressive behavior and other behavior problems. A strong body of research details the dangers of secondary smoke for children and also adults, especially if they are in situations (home, work) where they are getting a regular dose of secondary exposure.

And then there's tertiary exposure, which means exposure to traces of smoke that for years remain on the walls and other surfaces in the home, in the car, on parents' hair, and so on. It's less well studied than secondary smoking, but tertiary smoke exposure is known to have harmful physical effects on infants and children, increasing the risk for asthma and other respiratory diseases. The impact on behavior and learning is not yet clear, but some evidence suggests that tertiary smoke may impair a child's cognitive development (thinking) and ability to concentrate and be related to a greater risk of hyperactivity. In general, children are more likely to have behavior problems in a home where there is cigarette smoking or the products of cigarette smoking. Child rearing might be a little easier if this contextual influence were removed from your family's environment.

Deposits of lead, a heavy metal, accumulate in the body, including in the brain, and lead to serious physical health problems and in heavy doses even death. Lead exposure has all sorts of psychological effects that have been well documented. Children exposed to relatively low levels of lead show lower IQ scores and do more poorly on tasks involving math or reading, or that require concentration. They are more likely to be hyperactive and to experience mental retardation. Lead has been controlled pretty well in the United States in recent years and is much less of a problem than it once was. Lead-based paint, lead-lined plumbing, leaded-gas fumes from gas in cars, and other such sources have been limited. Still, some cans of food from foreign countries use lead, some imported

candies still have lead in the wrappers, and some ceramic contain-
ers, particularly from other countries, have lead that can leach into
food or drink taken from them.

What you can do
Obviously, it's essential to do your best to keep your child away from
cigarette smoke, lead, and other toxins. But is there anything positive to be said about biological factors that can help child rearing and
relate to children's behavior? Yes. For instance, studies have shown
that diets low in omega-3 fatty acids are related to psychological
problems, including depression and aggression. These fatty acids are
found in fish, such as salmon, tuna, and halibut; in other seafood,
including algae and krill (granted, algae and krill omelets are hard to
find in most restaurants); and in some plants and nut oils. They play
a major role in brain functioning, heart health, and normal growth
and development. In relation to behavior, evidence suggests that taking omega-3 supplements during pregnancy can increase a child's
mental processing ability and reduce discipline problems four years
after the child is born. The work is proceeding but it's still prelimi-
nary. Researchers are currently trying to determine the most effective
dose and whether there are any short- or long-term negative effects,
so we don't yet know enough about omega-3 fatty acids to advise
parents to take some pills and expect fewer discipline problems. No
one vitamin, mineral, or food trumps balance, moderation, and generally healthful eating.

8. Take care of yourself

Your need to take care of yourself isn't limited to a concern with your
effectiveness as a parent. But I mention it here, and in fact end this
chapter on context with it, because taking care of yourself is related
to your child's functioning in the home and provides an important
contextual influence.

It's easy to forget to keep yourself in good mental and physical
shape for child rearing. Parenting, running a household, working,

sustaining a relationship, and planning for multiple futures (your children's, your own, perhaps your parents') combine to put a lot of stress on you. The challenges keep coming at you—and coming back at you, because you can't ever settle any one of them for good and cross it off your list of things to do. You're in for a long haul, the proverbial marathon and not a sprint, and you're going to need to be in shape for it. Actually, it's more of a triathlon, with three potentially exhausting legs—childhood, adolescence, adulthood—and you have to be in shape for all three.

It's important that you see to your own needs, and not just your child's, by building in your own downtime, your own social interaction, your own special routines with your spouse or friends. This isn't "me generation" propaganda or "I come first" selfishness; it's what the research on parent-child interaction tells us about the best route to effective parenting. If you're flat-out all the time, you're going to break down, or at least show the negative effects of that stress in how you interact with your child. Invest a little of your energy in yourself; it will pay off for your family, and you'll also be modeling for your children the importance of taking care of oneself, a skill you want them to learn. As airplane safety instructions remind us, you'll be a lot more use to your loved ones if you put on your own oxygen mask before you help your children put on theirs.

What you can do

You are the best judge of what influences help you retain sanity in a complex world. One person may find sustenance and renewal in gardening, another in playing in a band, volunteering, or taking a long walk. You're a grownup; I won't presume to tell you how to take care of yourself. But, as a rough guide, think of each of the categories discussed in this chapter as applying to you, too. "Build positive social relations," for example, means that you should have at least one friend you can rely on, and if you don't, take the time to work on it a bit. Even from the narrow standpoint of equipping yourself for child rearing, it's time well invested. Quantity time with your child may be more important than quality time, but quantity time is not very useful if you are feeling isolated, depressed, stressed, impatient, or under the gun without an ally to turn to.

Conclusion

Context refers to broad, general influences on child rearing and development. I have saved them for last because they are not as useful in changing behavior when you have specific goals in mind such as getting your child to eat vegetables, to speak respectfully, to stop driving the downstairs neighbors crazy by jumping up and down on the floor, or to play gently with the dog. These and endless other areas of interest are readily addressed by the ABCs and your skill in using them.

The bigger-picture topics grouped in this chapter under the heading of context all represent influences that can powerfully affect the level of effort you have to expend on child rearing, the level of problem behaviors you have to deal with, and therefore your effectiveness in using the ABCs to get the results you want. Some of these connections of context and behavior change are easily seen. For example, if you don't take care of yourself (one of our contextual influences), your voice may be a little more stressed when you talk to your child, an antecedent for your child to not comply with your request to set the table for dinner (a request that, when you're under more stress, is more likely to come off as a command). Or, if a household is lacking in routines and tends toward chaos, bedtimes can fluctuate wildly, which means children are likely to be less well rested and more irritable and therefore less compliant with a parent's request to set the table. It's not accurate or useful to regard that noncompliance as the child's fault or as your fault—this is not about fault. It is about aligning the two sets of influences, the ABCs and context, to make child rearing easier.

I haven't even attempted to cover every significant contextual influence, and just because I didn't mention a specific aspect of context here doesn't mean that it's unimportant or unstudied in the scientific literature. The logic I followed in taking an admittedly partial pass through this chapter's vast subject matter was to focus on some major contextual influences that set the tone of the home, have been well studied by scientists, and are most likely to support and make more effective your use of ABCs. Keeping squarely in view that this book is about putting tools in the toolkit and using them effectively, I've let that priority guide me in my treatment of context.

6

The Kazdin Method

In Real Life

Throughout this book I've shown you how to use the ABCs and how to think about context to change your child's behavior and habits of mind. Your parenting toolkit is filled. Now I want to take you step by step through some behavior-change programs that apply the tools to the kinds of challenges that come up in everyday real-life settings. If you are wondering how to begin, which tool to pick up first, and how to lay out and complete the task, this chapter will help by giving you some examples that will serve as models for developing programs in your own home. Don't worry if your exact situation or problem isn't covered here. I'll concentrate on process, and my aim is to use these examples to help you set up your own programs to address your specific concerns. Before I get to the examples, let's start with a Kazdin Method blueprint, a summary of all the tools you can adapt to your own purposes.

The Kazdin Method blueprint

Step 1. Start by specifying the goal behaviors. What do you want your child to do?
Define what you want in specific terms. What is the behavior you

want to occur, and when? What would the behavior look like if it were exactly the way you wanted it to be? If you're interested in decreasing or eliminating some behavior, remember to specify and focus on the positive opposite.

It's valuable to write out exactly in a sentence or two what you want to see in your child. It's not as obvious as it sounds. A parent said to me, "I know when my kid eats vegetables at dinner: like never!" Yes, but in specifying the behavior, what will be the goal? Eating at least three forkfuls of vegetables? Eating all of the vegetables you serve him every night? Do some vegetables—say, fried potatoes—not count? Being specific makes a difference once we get to shaping and consequences. Fuzzy behavioral goals in the beginning can lead to very inconsistent reinforcement, so it pays to be specific up front. You can't specify everything that will come up, but try to paint a clear verbal picture of what the behavior you want looks like.

Step 2. Antecedents: How do you get the behavior going?

Use verbal prompts—clear statements, usually preceded by "please," with a positive (rather than authoritarian) tone, that specify exactly what you would like. The effectiveness of prompts is not increased by mere repetition; in fact, repetition decreases your effectiveness by making your prompts aversive.

You can use physical prompts, too, like gestures and modeling. You can, for instance, help the child with early parts of the behavior: "Let's do this together," or "Let's take turns; I can go first," or "Let's take turns and toss this coin to see who gets to go first" (a good addition of a little game or competition here).

You can also use setting events, which help set the stage for a behavior in addition to your use of prompts to specifically guide or instruct it. What is going on right before the behavior you want and leading up to that? Is there something you can control to make the behavior more likely? Well before bedtime, for instance, start some winding-down routine that is calm, quiet, leading to getting into bed. More generally, plan transitions from one activity to the next so that you're not springing abrupt changes or demands on your child if you can avoid it. Ask yourself, "If I want my child to do X soon, is what he's doing now a good or seamless transition to that?" If not, schedule something that sets a little better tone or platform for going to the next behavior.

If you feel it's likely that your child will resist what you're asking her to do, set the stage with some high-probability requests. These are requests she's likely to follow, like doing something with you, helping you, having a snack with you, anything that will not be perceived as a chore. High-probability requests can increase compliance with low-probability requests.

Give choices when you can because choice is a setting event that increases the likelihood of getting the behavior you would like. Even when there's no real choice to make — for example, homework has to be done before school tomorrow — there can still be choices along the way. "Would you like me to start the homework with you, or do you want to start on your own?" "Do you want to do the homework tonight at the kitchen table, while I'm preparing dinner, or in your room as usual?"

Finally, a challenge is a great setting event. For young children, a playful "I'll bet you can't . . ." can be a very effective setting event that motivates behavior and increases the likelihood of getting the behavior you wish.

Step 3. Behaviors: What can you do to get to the final behaviors you want?

Think of the final behavior you want. What would you like the behavior to look like, as specified in Step 1? Write it down at the bottom of a blank sheet of paper. Now describe exactly what your child usually does right now. Write that down at the top. Think of these two lines you've written as the first and last of a list of steps. The top of the list, the first line, is what your child is doing now — say, no homework, and she won't even sit at her desk. The last line, the bottom of the list, is the final behavior that you want — forty-five minutes of homework in which the child is sitting at her desk at home, without having to be told, doing schoolwork assigned by the teacher.

Now consider shaping as inserting into the list some intermediate steps between the top of the list (nada) and the bottom (the final behavior). We want to shape the child's behavior in such a way that we systematically move from what the child does now to the next step (say, sitting down with homework in front of her for a minute), and the next (doing a few minutes of homework), and so on to the final behavior. Shaping will develop the behavior systematically and consistently so that the program will not have to be in place forever.

Avoid the trap of saying to yourself, "My child already knows how to do this final behavior, even if she refuses to do it, so shaping isn't needed." Remember that knowing that something is true about a behavior—smoking is bad for you, donating to charity to help children is good, eating spinach and broccoli is really wise, being less sarcastic with my in-laws would be good—is only weakly related to one's actual behavior. The point of departure for shaping is beginning with what a person actually does now.

If the behavior you want never occurs or is very infrequent, set up simulations in which you can get the behavior you want under fake or pretend conditions. Make up a game (for example, the Tantrum Game) and use antecedents (prompts, modeling, setting events like playfulness and choice), shaping (ask for just a little at first), and consequences (spectacular praise). How do you decide whether to use shaping by itself or to set up simulations? As a rough guide, if the behavior does not occur once or twice a day in any form so it cannot be shaped, go to simulations for a week.

Sometimes the child has done a particular behavior (a chore, for instance, or a school assignment) in the past but has stopped or slacked off for some reason, and you just want him to start doing it again. Here is a case where the child really has done the behavior (rather than just knowing how to do it), so shaping is not needed—no need to develop the final behavior. Also, simulations aren't needed because the behavior does occur, if you could only get your child started on it again. This is where jump-starting can come in handy. You help the child with early steps, to just get started. If the behavior is doing homework and he can do that, go with him to start the first task—then you can leave or fade yourself out as he gets going on the homework. When you jump-start, you ask yourself, "What can I do positively just to prime the pump and get the behavior going?"

Helping with early steps can get the sequence of behavior going, and you can also use antecedents—a challenge, a choice—and then, of course, effusively praise starting without you.

Behavior is a key step because the goal of the program is to get the behavior to occur often, regularly, and consistently. Shaping, simulations, and jump-starting are valuable aids to getting the behavior to occur so that you can reinforce it—and reinforced practice is the key to success.

Step 4. Positive consequences: What positive consequences will you use to follow the behavior?

You want to provide a reinforcing consequence for the behavior you are developing. What are the consequences you can provide regularly when the behavior occurs? Praise is the default consequence to consider—your praise and attention are likely to be very powerful. Yet praise has to be delivered in a special way if it is to be used strategically to change behavior. You need to be enthusiastic, say what exactly you are praising, and then add something nonverbal like an affectionate touch or high-five.

Points and point charts can be used. Points are provided for behavior and are used to buy agreed-on rewards. To provide a point chart you need a medium of exchange (such as marks, stars, tallies), rewards that can be purchased by the points, and a list of what behaviors earn how many points and how many points are required to buy each reward. Points can be useful to help structure and organize your effort to change behavior, but they can be a distraction, too. The magic is not in the points at all. Even when you are awarding points, the praise and attention that come with them remain important. Keep in mind that your objective is reinforced practice, getting the behavior to occur and providing reinforcing consequences, and points are merely one of several types of consequences.

Step 5. Punishment: Is there any punishment that can be a constructive part of the program?

Punishment is not needed to change behavior in most settings. Also, remember that punishment does not teach a child what to do and only temporarily suppresses the behavior you're trying to eliminate. At the same time, I recognize that as a parent you will want to punish some behaviors that you just don't allow in your home. So, if you have to use it, make sure punishment is mild and brief. A few minutes of time out is just as effective as a longer period of time out; take away a privilege for the day or evening, not two weeks. Most critical of all, any time you punish a behavior, make sure you're reinforcing the positive opposite of that behavior more frequently. If you're not getting enough chances to reinforce the behavior you want, consider shaping or simulations.

Also, if you are going to use punishment, plan it in advance. How many minutes of time out do you give for talking back disrespectfully? Where? In your child's room? Somewhere else? And if your child does not go to time out right away, what privilege will you take away, and for how long? Also, what if you wish to use punishment while you're riding in the car or shopping, and time out is not possible? Choose a privilege in advance that you can withdraw in such situations. When they don't plan in advance, parents often select an unnecessarily harsh punishment in the heat of the moment, which greatly increases the likelihood of undesirable side effects.

There's also withholding reinforcement—not attending to misbehavior. To the extent possible, ignore and walk away from behaviors you don't like. Attention to behavior, even reprimands or other negative attention, can reinforce the very behaviors you wish to eliminate. It is important to make the point that not all reinforcers that maintain behavior are positive, lovely events. When you get mad, when you yell and scream and rage at your child, you're still providing more contact, giving more (negative) attention to a behavior—all of which could unwittingly be maintaining behavior because such attention works like positive reinforcement. No child would identify your angry reaction as a reward, but it's still a reinforcer (that's why psychologists distinguish between reinforcers and rewards; they're often but not always the same) because your negative response is still attention, which can sustain a behavior like oxygen feeds a fire.

Step 6. Do a quick check of context
The preceding steps address specific procedures to use in developing a behavior-change program. Yet the context, the more general background or atmosphere in which you use the tools in this book, is extremely important. Context can have a big effect on the behaviors you may want to change, and on your success in changing them. For example, if there is a major disruption in a child's routines and activities, or a stressful event such as a separation, move, change in schools or classrooms, or an illness in the family—any such event that disrupts a more stable context could easily lead to an increase in the child's misbehavior. In these cases the child's misbehaviors are a common part of adaptation and will come and go as the routine hits an unstable patch and then becomes more stable again. In these situations, focus on putting as many of the context pieces we have outlined back into place as you can. Often you can diminish behavioral problems by checking on context alone and doing what you can to reestablish a familiar routine. Remember that the list includes promoting good communication with your child; building positive family connections; promoting positive social behavior; fostering flexibility in your household; monitoring your child—knowing where he is, whom he's with, what he's doing; minimizing negative social, psychological, and biological conditions for your child; and taking care of yourself.

Real-life applications

Let's apply the steps more concretely to real children and real programs from the Yale Parenting Center.

Real life No. 1: Rory, a three-year-old who has mastered the word no
Rory is a three-year-old boy who lives at home with two older brothers who are in elementary school. The mother and father report that Rory never complies with what they ask. He doesn't come down to dinner when called, get ready for bed, get dressed to go to the store,

take a nap, or do anything else they ask him to do. The parents have heard about the "terrible twos" but did not experience them with their other sons when they were Rory's age. (The "terrible twos" usually refers to not listening rather than to tantrums and other, more serious misbehavior like fighting or destroying things, and when the so-called terrible twos do emerge, it usually happens at about age three.) All of a sudden it seems as if Rory has a will of his own, and his parents don't know how to manage him. In many such cases, parents become more forceful, a little harsher, and a little more insistent on being listened to. They often feel it's important to set limits and make clear who's in charge. That's understandable, but the usual method employed by parents is a show of strength, and that's an antecedent for more resistance and less compliance.

We begin with the first step of asking what the parents would like to see—the goal behaviors of the program we are to develop. They don't just want Rory to stop saying no all the time; they want him actually to do what they ask. We decide together that the positive opposite of saying no and not doing what they ask is to comply with their requests. We're shooting for consistency here, not perfection. I point out just as background that even the best-behaved children comply only about 80 percent of the time when asked to do something. We don't have parallel research on adults, but probably spouses, partners, colleagues, friends, relatives, and others do not comply all the time either. And if that doesn't persuade you to lighten up a little, remember that we do not even comply with our own instructions to ourselves (think: New Year's resolutions). So, although we won't insist on perfection, we have the goal behavior down: doing what is asked—within a minute of being asked, in fact, just to keep it precise.

Further discussion with the parents reveals that Rory sometimes does comply with requests. That's important to know because if the behavior occurs a little, we can easily build on that. Remember, if the behavior never, ever occurs, we might have to do simulations just to get it going. But it turns out Rory goes to the bathroom and brushes his teeth with his parents before going to bed, then goes to bed, then asks for a story and listens to it. Also, after some meals with the family he is asked to clear his place, as his brothers do, and he does that, too. So we have some positive-opposite good behavior to work with.

Let's consider antecedents. We already know the behavior occurs, but we want to check if there are antecedents that could be used better. Are there some antecedents that are interfering with compliance? I ask the parents to pretend I'm Rory and to tell me to do something, especially something Rory is likely to refuse to do. The mother asks me to get my jacket because we're going to the store. She looks me in the eye and holds up one finger on her right hand about chest high and points not at me or straight up but somewhere in between and says, "Rory—get your jacket; we are going to the store." This is a reasonable prompt, but it's easy to tell the mom is battle-worn. She's ready for noncompliance and has, understandably, already loaded her next response ready to fire when needed. We can help here. The prompt is good in content, clearly directing a specific behavior, but it could be improved in the setting-event parts. I ask her not to make any gestures with her finger. The pointing could decrease the likelihood of compliance because it adds a little look of force or authority. Also, her matter-of-fact, neutral tone is not bad, but it could be better. I ask her to smile as she speaks (to help control the pleasantness of tone). Finally, I ask her to begin the prompt with "please." All of these accompaniments to the prompt make compliance more likely.

She asks, "I have to do all of this just to get him to comply?" I assure her that it's just for a little while. Then I pretend she is Rory and say, with a gentle tone, no pointing, a smile, and "please," "Rory, please put on your jacket; we're going to the store. I can help you if you would like." Doing something with the child to help the behavior along is a nonverbal prompt. Giving Rory a choice (help if he would like) increases the likelihood of compliance. Also, actually helping him would be a prompt that could easily be faded later.

Still on antecedents, I mention that once in a while she can precede her prompt with a comment like "Rory, this might be hard to do. It's something you will be able to do easily when you're a bigger boy, but let's try just for the heck of it," after which she can go into her regular prompt, as we've practiced. This big-boy comment, a gentle challenge (as I discussed in chapter one), is a very important setting event that increases the likelihood he will comply.

Now to consequences. Rory does in fact comply with many of his parents' requests. The parents, like the rest of us, they tend to let the good responses go unnoticed and focus on the noncompliance. For a little while, we need to change this.

We ask the parents to find at least three opportunities each day to praise an instance in which Rory did listen and did what they wanted. There is no magic in the number three, but we give this as a minimum. Reinforced practice (occurrence of the behavior followed by praise) is the central concept, and we want repeatedly to connect behavior to positive consequences for compliance.

The father asks the reasonable question "Why praise him for something he's already doing?" The answer is that we want to increase compliance in all situations, and so for a little while we want to praise all compliance. It will spill over and improve compliance in the situations where Rory may now say no.

In addition to an increase in praise for compliance, we want to single out those instances when Rory has been likely to say no. If Rory complies with one of those requests, the parent's praise should be ecstatic. "I cannot *believe* you did that just like a big boy!" Now, if your spouse or someone else is around, bring that person into the room and tell him all about the amazingly excellent behavior. As that other adult enters the room, say, "Wait until you hear this: 'big boy' Rory did . . . exactly as I asked and right away! Can you believe it?" and the other adult will no doubt jump in, grasping the letter and spirit of the exercise, and that praise will further help. If all of this feels over the top, too much, and unnecessary—remember, it's all temporary while we're developing behavior, and these early steps are important and will help. And remember, also, that Rory is three, which means that over-the-top enthusiasm when his parents praise him will greatly increase their chances of success.

What if a child does not comply with a request? This is very likely to occur as we are developing behavior; we will not jump from a little to complete compliance. And, as I noted, even angelic children (or adults) do not comply all the time. If the request isn't urgent (say, getting out of the house for a doctor's appointment) and you can walk away from him if he says no, that would be one option. More likely the parent can provide a mild form of punishment. "OK, if you won't get dressed, I will dress you, and you lose fifteen minutes of your TV show tonight"—or "you get no dessert," or something equivalent. Be calm and nonpunitive in your tone, and if you have to dress him, do not do it harshly as if you are mad. That will lead to side effects, among them your getting hit in the face.

More focused consequences (better praise for compliance) and better antecedents should reduce the frequency of "no" and increase Rory's compliance. But there could well be one or two important areas that are still not improved. There are further options, such as simulation of these two areas in a game that earns points. For example, if Rory is still very difficult about taking a nap, his parents can set up a game in which he can earn points by getting ready to take a nap in a simulated situation (that is, they play the game when it's not really nap time), then cash in those points for a small extra reward or privilege: a chance to reach in a grab bag of little prizes, ten minutes of extra time before going to bed, that kind of thing. Alternatively, they can tell Rory that there are Special Rory Challenges. These are the requests for him to do the tasks he still finds it more difficult to comply with, like getting ready to take a nap. Before they ask him to do one of these, they say, "OK, here comes a Special Rory Challenge," then prompt as usual. When he complies in these situations, they of course lavish praise on him, but also add a special reward. Usually this won't be needed, but the term Special Rory Challenge is an antecedent that will mark these situations nicely for Rory, and the extra or special consequence can bring these around if they have not otherwise led to compliance.

Real life No. 2: Emma, a six-year-old who has perfected dawdling

Emma is a six-year-old in the first grade. She lives at home with her mother, father, and four-year-old brother. Emma's mom really wants help with her child's dawdling. Emma has trouble getting ready for anything—for school, her dance lesson on Saturdays, appointments of any kind, and just going to the grocery store. The most important, frustrating, and frequent situation in which this occurs is getting ready for school each weekday morning. She has not mastered "getting ready," although her mother has explained several times that "*ready* means that in the morning you are down here at the table, sitting, ready to eat breakfast so you can get to school on time. What part of that don't you understand?" Understanding is not, of course, the issue. It's a behavior problem.

The first step is to select the behaviors we want to develop and define them clearly. We will work eventually with more than one of the situations, but we pick one to begin with. Doing that will allow us to focus and achieve some change, and to make sure the procedures are effective and implemented carefully. Also, if Emma improves her ability to get ready in one situation (say, school-day mornings), the effect will spread on its own to other situations (say, before ballet on Saturdays) and we will not have to focus on each one in turn.

So we focus on her getting down to breakfast on time on school days. Emma's mom wants her downstairs at about 7:25, ready to eat breakfast, which is usually waiting for her on the table. She wants Emma to eat and be ready for the school bus, which arrives between 7:50 and 8:00. Once the bus pulls up, the driver waits no more than a minute before driving off. (When Emma misses the bus, her mom has to drive her to school and then drive in the opposite direction to take her brother to daycare.)

I ask a little more about the behavior. What, exactly, happens now? I ask this for two reasons. First, I want to see "where Emma is," because knowing what she already does will be a starting point for selecting where to begin shaping. Second, I want to check on all the antecedents because it's likely we could do a lot there to help get the desired behavior. I learn that the mom wakes Emma up at about 6:50 and asks her to get dressed. Then the mom is back and forth from the kitchen to Emma's bedroom upstairs several times to push her along verbally with prompts: "Come on, get dressed, what are you doing now? Don't dawdle!" This continues, with everyone growing more tense and peeved, until Emma gets downstairs at about 7:35 or 7:40, backpack in hand, gobbles some cereal, and is semi-gently pushed out the door while her mom hands her a lunch bag pretty much the way relay sprinters pass the baton. If Emma eats breakfast, has all her stuff for school, and is out the door by the time the bus pulls up, that's a "good day" scenario, although even on a good day her mom is already drained from the struggle to keep Emma on schedule. And on bad days, of course, the baton gets dropped and the morning implodes.

So here is our program. The goal is for Emma to get ready without her mom coming into the room and directing her so much. Having her mom constantly going in and out of the room will at best get Emma out the door on time, but only for one day at a time; it will not teach her to do the behavior without heavy pressure, and the cost is too great: having to keep the pressure on really wears out her mother before the mother's day has even had a chance to begin. We want to decrease the antecedents (prompts) because there are way too many, and we want to change their tenor (the mom's voice is usually tense, full of urgency and hurry). We want the mom to be calm, say "please" before the prompt, and prompt less.

On the behavior side, shaping is definitely needed. We want Emma downstairs on time all ready to eat breakfast and then to go out the door. We can break down all of this into parts. We will focus on three. First, being dressed and downstairs on time. To shape that we will reinforce any approximations of being ready (for example, partially dressed) but provide special rewards if Emma does more than that and is ready on time. Second, we will focus on two component behaviors separately: having her backpack ready for school and having her clothes ready to put on in the morning. We can work on both of these behaviors by having Emma complete them the night before. So on Sunday night, for example, she can earn praise and another incentive if she has her backpack all packed and ready to go for Monday morning and also if she has her clothes picked out and ready to put on in her room. Emma working on these the night before serves as jump-starting, or priming, the behavior of getting ready the next morning. That is, we have her already engaging in getting-ready behaviors the night before, so when she wakes up, she's already a few steps into the morning routine.

On the consequences side, we'll use praise for any of the steps that are completed, but we'll add a point chart to help Emma's parents. The point chart will be a simple sheet of paper marked with horizontal and vertical lines. Under the heading for each behavior, the mom will put an X whenever Emma earns a point for doing it. Next to the chart is a list of what the Xs earn: 2 Xs = dessert at dinner or an extra story read by Mom or Dad before bedtime, or a Wii game with her brother before dinner; 3 Xs = play with Mom's iPad (which is entirely off limits now) under Mom's supervision, or stay up fifteen minutes later on Friday or Saturday night; 5 Xs = a toy grab bag (Emma closes her eyes, reaches into a brown paper bag, and picks one toy from those that are in there); 15 Xs = a weekend movie at a movie theater, a trip to a nearby amusement park, or going fishing at a nearby pier. Emma helped make this list. Her parents asked her what were some things she would like to do, so they're confident that these are rewards she's eager to get.

When the parents present the program to Emma, they tell her there's a way for her to earn some things she would like by getting ready on time. There are two ways to earn points. First, there's "night-before prep." She can earn one point on any school night (Sunday through Thursday) if she has her backpack downstairs before bedtime on the kitchen counter all ready to go to school. She can earn another point if she has the clothes she's going to wear (shoes, socks, the outfit) all laid out on or by her dresser in her room before bedtime. Her dad helps her do this for the first week, just to help her get the idea and into the routine. Also, getting ready partially in this way removes much of the tension. There is no time pressure at night, and there will be less the next morning. Time pressure is a setting event for oppositional behavior, so it's good to reduce or eliminate it.

In the morning Emma can earn two points if she's completely dressed by 7:25 *and* if her mom has to remind Emma to get dressed only once. If Emma is not dressed by 7:25, the mom finishes dressing her and Emma doesn't get any points. Mom will praise partial dressing or showing other progress toward getting dressed ("It's good you picked out your clothes and put them on your bed," for instance, or "I can see you are almost all dressed—very good!"), so it's not an all-or-nothing scenario, but Emma gets the points only if both criteria are met. This is absolutely critical. In developing behavior (via praise in this case) one reinforces any approximations or improvements in behavior. So here we are praising partial dressing and getting close, but we save points and even more effusive praise for when the final behavior is achieved. This is the best of all worlds—praise for improvement and a special incentive for actually doing the desired behavior completely.

On Sunday evening, the program officially starts. Emma's dad agrees to be in charge of the "night-before prep" phase. He goes to her right after dinner, way before bedtime, and says, "Let's earn some Emma points" and holds her hand as they walk to her room. (Hand holding on the way is a nice setting event to get the behavior requested.) Then he says, "You can get a point if you get your backpack all ready and we take it down to the kitchen so it's there to grab on your way to the school bus." (Mentioning the point is a setting event that will increase the likelihood of the behavior.) He asks her to show him exactly what she needs to do to get the backpack ready, since he doesn't know. Emma puts a few things in, describing each step out loud, and the dad thanks her for explaining—all great to keep the tone positive. He praises her for doing this so quickly. "Great, Emma—you got this all ready so fast! How did you do that?" he says with an expression of pride and amazement, and then rubs the back of her head gently. Then he says, "Let's go downstairs to put it on the counter for tomorrow morning." As soon as she does that, the dad takes her over to the point chart and marks an X—gives her some praise, a hug, and says, "You're pretty good at this for just the first time; did you practice when I wasn't looking?" If Emma smiles and is proud of herself, which she's likely to be, that's all to the good.

The dad says, "We can stop here, or if you want we can work on the clothes and get them ready for tomorrow. You'll get a point for that, but we don't have to do that now if you don't want to." Dad nicely uses choice here as a setting event to increase the likelihood of compliance. He could have said, "Emma, now we have to get your clothes ready." That wording is a little less desirable here because "have to" increases the likelihood of an "over my dead body or in your dreams" reaction on Emma's part. If Emma does the clothes, too, there's more praise and another trip to the refrigerator to add a point to her chart.

Why not do the backpack upstairs and while up there just do the clothes and save the extra trip up and down stairs? Because, at first, two trips are better. One behavior occurs (backpack) and then it gets its immediate reward (trip to the point chart), then the other behavior occurs (clothes) and gets its own immediate reward (trip to the point chart). Also, doing it this way circumvents the problem that would come up if Emma does only one of the two tasks and the dad then has to mix praise and points with a comment like "Well, maybe next time you can get a point for getting your clothes ready, too." In the beginning, take one behavior and its consequence at a time. When both behaviors are consistent, it then becomes efficient to award points for both with one trip to the point chart after both are done. In fact, to make that transition one could even use a challenge as a setting event. "All right, Emma, you've been doing the backpack and clothes really well, but here's the challenge. Can you do them both one right after the other before we go downstairs and do the points? You will still get all your points, but doing two things in a row—that's pretty hard" (said playfully). "You want to try"—choice—"or is it just too hard?"—challenge. Emma will probably move to two in a row, and Dad can praise that. "You really *are* good at this," and then he states exactly what the "this" is and touches her shoulder gently.

In the morning, the mom awakens Emma as usual and gives a calm reminder after an affectionate good morning. "OK, you can earn some more points if you like. Please get dressed and come to the kitchen by 7:25." There's a clock in Emma's room and Emma can tell time. "If you want any help, just call me. That's fine for this first week. If you come down completely dressed by 7:25 or I come up and see you are dressed, you get two points. If you are not dressed by then, I will dress you to make sure we get the school bus on time. If I dress you, you won't get any points."

For the first three or four days, Emma's dad helps her with the night-before prep. Then they try a challenge: "I'll bet you can't do this on your own. Let's see." Here Emma is being asked to go to her room and do both behaviors. Dad says to Emma, "Call me to come up when you're ready for me to see." When Emma has done both behaviors, the dad goes upstairs, praises, and they come down to get the points. He tells Emma she's so big and mature in doing this, she gets to mark the "prep" points on the chart herself. Throughout all of this, the parents put the emphasis on praising Emma each night for getting the backpack ready and getting her clothes together without any help.

In the first week Emma gets completely dressed by 7:25 on three days but not completely dressed on two days. On those two less successful days, the mom looks for reasons to praise Emma when she comes into Emma's room at 7:25: "Great, you're almost completely dressed! I can't give you points today, but you have another chance tomorrow. It's so great that you were almost all dressed. What a big girl!" Praise for approximations of the behavior is important for shaping. Praise for trying and for partial success is also good.

After doing the program for a while, Emma has getting ready in the morning down, and she's consistently doing the two behaviors the night before. Also, on most of the days she comes down dressed and on time, or a minute or two early. The mom and dad make a big deal of this with their praise. They already have faded themselves—that is, they don't have to be present in the moment as a setting event to get the behavior or as a prompt to help. Now it's time to get rid of the points.

They say, "You're such a big girl you don't even need points to help you do this. We're going to add something special on Friday or Saturday. At the end of any week when you have come down every morning on time ready to go to school, you can choose either a dinner and dessert you want at home on Friday or a family activity on Saturday." If she's not ready on one day, Mom still goes up and finishes dressing her. Emma still gets praise for doing things well, even partially well, but no more points—just praise, and that special activity when she has been ready on time every morning for a solid week. The special activity is very delayed as a reinforcer, which is fine after behavior is well established.

Pretty soon Emma has all of this down as a habit—she is getting ready on time, routinely, and not under the control of parents or points. The point program is dropped and the Friday or Saturday event is done only the first week, after which everyone kind of loses track of that loose program. That's all fine, too. You have to be very systematic in the beginning and then can be loose as a way of fading the program—just the way we are naturally loose as years go by in not reminding our child to say "thank you," to use a napkin rather than a sleeve, to say "I'm sorry" when an apology is needed.

Real life No. 3: Logan's school behavior has the teacher on his parents' case

Logan is a nine-year-old boy who is doing pretty well in the fourth grade. He's in middle reading and math groups and has some friends; overall, he's doing fine. He lives with his mom and younger sister; the mother and father were divorced two years ago, and Logan and his sister see their dad one day on the weekends, and they sometimes stay overnight. The mother has a mail-order business buying and selling merchandise through eBay and works at home.

It's mid-October when the mother comes to the Yale Parenting Center. After six weeks of the new school term, the teacher is starting to call or send e-mails two or three times a week. Apparently Logan is disrupting others and getting into trouble for talking during work or study time and not doing what he's supposed to do. The mother, in disbelief, tells us that he has been sent to a detention room three times already in a two-week period. That and the teacher's many calls mean the mother can't just let it go for now. She's under pressure to deal with the problem.

The teacher's calls include the reminder that she has twenty-three other students to attend to, that she can't do anything special for Logan because of that, and that the mom needs to take care of this. To make sure mother anxiety is high, the teacher says that if this keeps up, she will recommend Logan for special education class placement where someone else can deal with his disruptive behavior.

The mother feels that the pressure's on her, but that she's not in a good position to deal with the problem. "I'm not at school," she says. "What can *I* do to help?" She has told Logan to behave or else there will be more problems for him at school. It's understandable that she's been driven to making those statements, but predictably they have no real effect on changing Logan's behavior. (They are poor prompts—distant from the situation, not followed with reinforcement for engaging in the right behavior—and will have no effect on changing behavior. They also can increase Logan's anxiety, which will not motivate him to behave better. And even if they did motivate him, great motivation alone does not lead to behavior change if that behavior is not well developed in the child's repertoire.) We can adapt our tools to this situation, I tell her.

But first, to get the whole picture, what exactly is the behavior? We look at the teacher's list of disruptive behaviors and ask her (by e-mail) if there are other things to add to that. There's one: sometimes Logan blurts out things in class without raising his hand, and that's disruptive and unfair to others who do raise their hands. And with that addition we pretty much have the behavior down.

Because the consequences part of this program is a little novel, let's go to that and come back to antecedents and behaviors in a moment. I tell the mom that because the teacher has too many children to attend to and can't give Logan the one-on-one attention necessary to carry out a full behavior-change program in school, we are going to do a *home-based reinforcement program*. It has two main parts:

1. A token economy (point chart) set up at home. Logan can earn points each day based on his performance in class. We give points for behavior, which I'll come to in a moment. The points can be exchanged for things that Logan would like. The mom consults Logan and he lists these rewards: staying up half an hour later on a weeknight and one hour later on a weekend night, more computer time, cooler (colored) sneakers to replace his white ones (which no one else on the planet

supposedly wears), baseball cards, Pokémon cards, rental of a video game, and a cell phone. The mother agrees to all except the cell phone. Point values are calibrated so that some things can be earned easily: two to three points earns staying up late; three points for fifteen minutes more computer time (computer is restricted in the home and the computer is in the family room where it can be supervised); five points for a pack of baseball cards; and so on. There are also bigger items for which Logan has to save: ten points for a (nonviolent) video game; fifty points for cooler sneakers.

2. A way of measuring behavior to determine how many points Logan earns.

Each weekday, Logan takes a white 3-by-5-inch card to school. On the cards are three smiley-type faces, each next to a number: 2 has a very cheery smiley face and means that Logan had a really good day with very little or almost no disruptive behavior; 1 has a gently smiling face and means that Logan was a little disruptive and was not really great but not out of control or horrible; and 0 has a neutral flat-mouth face and means that Logan was pretty disruptive. (The mom bought sheets of smiley faces at a party store, but just drawing them would be fine, too.) There's a sheet at home and one e-mailed to the teacher to define what behaviors rate a 2, 1, or 0.

The mother asks the teacher to circle the 2, 1, or 0 on the 3-by-5 card, initial it, and send it home with Logan each day. The teacher feels that she can easily do that. If for some reason the card does not get scored, the teacher agrees to respond to an e-mail from Logan's mom.

The program is simple. Each day, Logan earns one point just for bringing home the card and handing it to his mom—for participating, in other words. He earns two more points if the teacher circled 2, one more point if 1, and no more points if the teacher circled 0. He loses a point if he starts arguing with his mom or the teacher about points earned that day, the way a baseball player can get kicked out of the game for arguing with the ump about a called strike. After his mom looks at the card (as soon as Logan comes home from school), marks (they could be stars, check marks, or some other symbol) are added to a chart on the wall that notes his points for the day and total points left in his account (total points minus any purchases). After the points are entered, Logan can cash in by identifying something he wants, or just let the points ride.

We are still on consequences. The mother asks the teacher to praise Logan any time he gets a 2 or a 1, but the real praise comes from the mother when Logan arrives home with a 2 or a 1 on his card. Yes, she praises a 1 (that's shaping), although she praises a 2 more strenuously. If Logan receives a 0, she gives him the point on the chart for bringing the card home and says in a calm, matter-of-fact tone, "Tomorrow is another chance, and you may earn more points then." (It's important to keep this brief, not to interrogate: "What did you do to make the teacher circle 0?" All such comments undermine the program; they're setting events that are inherently confrontational and will promote escape and avoidance, which could nix the program if Logan begins refusing to bring the card home.)

On her own, the mother adds something special when Logan receives a 2. She calls it a "2 treat licorice" because it's given for a 2 and the two of them eat it together. She keeps some licorice around for them to have whenever there's a 2 on the card. This is not needed in the program, but it's a nice addition to make a 2 extra special and to speed up shaping a little with an extra incentive for excellent behavior. Also, besides the licorice as reinforcer (and yes, I know, you can't use sweets as reinforcers too much and we do not advocate or rely on them at the Parenting Center), it's also parent-child time together to celebrate good behavior.

On the antecedents front, on the way to school the mother provides a gentle reminder as she hands Logan the card: "Good luck today in earning points; I'm thinking about you and I hope you can do it. It's hard to do, and don't feel too bad if you can't get all the points today." This is more of a setting event than a prompt (which would be more direct: "Remember, pay attention, do not blurt out . . ."), and it takes some of the pressure off, which increases the likelihood that Logan will do what's asked of him.

On the behavior front, shaping is key. After the first week, Logan is doing pretty well with mostly 1s and 2s. We ask the mother to add one extra bonus point any time Logan has two consecutive days of 2 on the card. So if on both Monday and Tuesday he has a 2, he gets the usual points for that and also a special bonus point. Then on Wednesday, he has a 2 again and so again receives a bonus point—because Tuesday and Wednesday were two 2 days in a row. This practice of adding a special incentive for consistency could be stretched out to three days in a row and so on, but it's best to proceed slowly to be sure the early steps are stable.

This sort of home-based reinforcement program is useful for school behavior problems. We have also used this kind of program for athletic practices, day camp, and other such situations where we can't ask the adult in charge to stick to a special program like administering praise for positive opposites on any regular basis that would have a significant effect. Asking a teacher or other supervising adult to fill out a card is reasonable and effective. In some recent cases, we've omitted the card and had teachers or others text the parent at the end of the day. But we prefer a physical card because it's tangible feedback that the child can touch and see.

Real life No. 4: Olivia's jarring irritability and attitude
Olivia, a twelve-year-old girl, is not especially physically or socially mature for her age. She still looks like a girl, while some of her peers are starting to be more shapely as they mature physically. This is what Olivia's parents mention when I see them. They kind of like her immaturity and late development; they are not in a rush to have an adolescent in the home. One girl in Olivia's class is already dating, and another has been caught by the teacher while sexting, which makes Olivia's parents shudder. They are waiting with dread for the first sign of adolescence in their daughter, the first shoe to drop, but they talk about it as if it's a guillotine, not a shoe, that will be dropping. They have come to the Yale Parenting Center because they think it's all just beginning, and in a way they didn't expect.

For starters, the family is close, engages in many family activities, has all sorts of good routines about meals, weekend activities, occasional field trips, and periodic vacations. So a lot of the contextual influences are already in place and positive. Olivia and her eight-year-old sister get along well; there's no real sibling rivalry, competition, or routine tension. But now, at age twelve, Olivia's showing a change in personality around the house. She's irritable much of the time and acts as if living at home with her parents is a prison sentence for a crime she did not commit. She does not go after her younger sister much, but she freely tells her parents that they are selfish and don't really love her; loses her temper and makes cutting remarks; and says that she doesn't want any of whatever is being served for dinner, even when her mother buys and prepares a favorite food — which, Olivia notes emphatically, she doesn't like anymore.

When offered a special treat that she's enjoyed before or invited to go someplace with her mother just to be together, where a light "No, thank you" would have done the job, now she replies with a stretched-out, sarcastic "Nooooooo," wagging her head and adopting a pained facial expression that conveys the ridiculous stupidity of the question. Acting lessons could never have perfected this level of irritability and dismissiveness, and the parents wonder where she got it and why. In addition, Olivia's obvious irritability casts a dark cloud over the dinner table. Conversation becomes stilted, and both Mom and Dad are tense and moody because of something nasty that Olivia just said or no doubt will soon say.

Before I address how to change this pattern of behavior, I tell the parents that irritability in adolescence is common. It's not inevitable, but it does occur. In young girls, other things can come on as well, like poor body self-image, lower self-esteem, more depression (which includes increased irritability), and, in more extreme cases, talk of self-harm and suicide. Small doses of each of these can occur; in their extreme they warrant seeing a professional. But this irritability is common and includes the mindset that "if my parents want this, do this, or think this, I don't want any part of it."

It would be nice merely to say to parents, "Sit tight; this will pass." But if you are in the home and a verbal mortar is aimed at you much of the day, you can't let it pass. You will have shell shock from all the bombardment, and some of the comments will be direct hits on your soul. And there's no need to put up with it.

A little praise program is not likely to do the trick. Praise will be included, but we want more powerful rewards that are not usually needed. We choose a point program here.

What behavior do we want? We want to focus on just one to begin with, but the parents insist that there's a whole suite of problem behaviors and any one of them could come up at any time. It will not be great for their morale to control eye rolling or sarcastic tone if in the next minute they're told to shut up or that no one really cares what they think, offenses that they will then feel obliged to punish severely. So we list all the behaviors of concern and take them all on in one program. How can we take on many behaviors and still use shaping? Hold on.

In terms of antecedents, what can we do to influence the likelihood that Olivia won't erupt in obnoxious behavior? The parents have already tried being kind and sweet, trying to show empathy or understanding, being harsh in return ("You'd better get control of your mouth and attitude"), and tiptoeing around Olivia in the hope that they won't set her off. We decide to try other antecedents.

The parents tell her, "It's fine to be upset and obnoxious around the house. Lots of teens go through that. There will be consequences when you cross the line into serious disrespect and meanness, but you can choose what to say or do." This antecedent does not feed the problem but removes all fighting and coercion, and that can decrease some of the irritability. The setting event disarms Olivia a bit by saying, in effect, "Your behavior is understandable, even normal, and we expect it." Also, such a disarming comment conveys that there are limits, so understanding and legitimizing her teen behavior is not a carte blanche to misbehave. It also decreases futile extended parent-child exchanges. (It is useful here to be disarming and matter-of-fact, without condescending with words or tone that might convey the equivalent of "You are just an immature brat and we are having as much trouble putting up with you as you are with us." Hold that thought for the parent support group that should be available for free to every parent raising an adolescent who is going through a bumpy period of development.) I tell the parents not to make the mistake of worrying that they're being weak or not setting limits. Actually, they're being quite strong by controlling the situation much better, and the program sets very effective limits.

Second, the parents draw up a list of annoying teen behaviors that they're concerned about and put it in a kitchen drawer where Olivia can see it any time she wants to. It's not posted on the refrigerator, which could embarrass the hyper-touchy Olivia, but everyone knows where it is and can get to it.

Now, as to the behavior itself, we definitely want to use shaping. We base shaping on time—that is, the amount of time Olivia goes without exhibiting one of these teen behaviors. If she can do that, she can earn points for all sorts of things she would like. The amount of time will change as she makes progress, of which more in a moment.

Consequences consist of a few things. She can earn points and exchange them for items like cosmetics, which she likes a great deal, and privileges like cell phone time, iTunes, TV time, and loosening of the parents' strict rules on makeup. This loosening is good for contextual reasons, too. The parents will need to start yielding more as Olivia's life will increasingly be outside her family and in the world. Tightening up and taking up slippery-slope thinking here can foster a lot more oppositional teen behavior, more time out of the home, and more time ignoring deeply ingrained but often hard-to-see household values. Loosening where you can (allowing more latitude in hairstyle and color of fingernails, for instance, or putting up with louder and perhaps coarser music than you'd normally want in the house) helps you to hold firm where you can't loosen up (for example, no tattoos, no music that includes foul language or promotes what you regard as terrible values).

Also, the parents offer low-key (rather than effusive) praise almost any time Olivia speaks decently to them. When she says something pleasant or at least minimally civil, the mom goes over to her and says something like "It's good to have another adult in the home—you! You are speaking so nicely," and then she gives her a thumbs-up and goes on about her business. The parent shouldn't linger in this situation, which could go downhill fast. One adolescent at the Parenting Center would say, "I don't need your f'in praise!" We can be pretty sure that means the praise was not rewarding (as subjectively valued by the recipient), but, still, it definitely was a positive reinforcer, and the adolescent's behavior changed in that case without any point program. A parent can barely resist responding to such provocative comments—so better to leave the exchange as soon as possible.

Finally, the parents use withholding reinforcement. The mother's reaction in particular often makes Olivia's teen behaviors have more monumental impact than they should. Yet there are times when her parents can't just ignore Olivia, so we practice a low-key reaction with the mother. She smiles slightly, a kind of Mona-Lisa-plus-just-a-little-expression that we practice with parents at the Parenting Center, and then walks away. The smile, which communicates a certain faint amusement at the daughter's fumbling efforts to get her mother's goat, as if to say, "Ah, yes, I was twelve once," is mildly aversive because it's a little dismissive, so it qualifies as a punishment. Mild punishment is all right as part of a program that strongly reinforces the positive opposites of the behavior that's being punished.

The program: The parents tell Olivia that she's growing up and so there are going to be changes in the home. They make a list of the various irritable things Olivia says and does in the home, and they put it where she can get it out and look at it, but she doesn't have to. They tell her that these irritable behaviors will go away as she becomes a young woman. It's OK for her to be irritable because she might not be able to control it, but if she can control her irritability and not do what's on the list, she can earn things like cosmetics, privileges, and other things she wants.

Here's how we'll do it. When Olivia comes home from school, she can be as irritable as she wants to be and do the behaviors on the list. But if she goes ten minutes without doing any of those things on the list, she earns five points. That can happen each day. Here's the catch: she has to say something to her parents, even if it's only "Hi," rather than just hiding in her room to let the ten minutes elapse. After the ten minutes, Olivia can do all the irritable "teen behaviors" she wants. (That antecedent of calling them "teen behaviors" and giving her free rein to do them is very likely to decrease the behaviors, too.) Over time the ten minutes is extended. Whenever Olivia has a lapse and does something on the list during the period when she can earn points for not doing it, the mom or dad just smiles and walks off slowly. If Olivia asks, "Well, did I get the damn points?" the parent replies, calmly, "Not today, but you have another chance tomorrow," and walks away.

One more feature: Saturday is a free day on which the program is suspended—no demands to act more grown-up, and no points can be earned. This is a smart addition because it gives freedom and takes pressure off. Also, this will help later, when Olivia's behavior has improved in long enough stretches that the family can make the transition from awarding points to just reinforcing good behavior with praise and attention. Olivia's parents tell her that she should feel free to do the "teen behaviors" on the free day if she wants to or can't help it. Legitimizing "teen behaviors" is an antecedent that takes some of the enjoyment (reward value) out of them; it also helps the parents to control their reactions, which can fuel continued obnoxious behavior.

Summing up

The four real-life examples I've just gone through are different in the behaviors they focus on, the ages of the children, and the circumstances. Yet they outline programs that can be individualized to your child, preteen, or adolescent. We know this because similar applications have been successfully adapted to toddlers, college and professional athletes, soldiers in basic training, employees in business and industry, the elderly, and others. So if you are thinking that this approach will never work with your child or that it can't be applied to this or that behavior, chances are you are wrong. (I admit that telling a person that she or he is wrong is a bad antecedent and is quite likely to evoke opposition to what I have just said.)

Right or wrong, try your way first, and then try the toolkit this book offers, only if your first attempt did not work to your satisfaction. Consider the toolkit as your backup when you want to develop a new behavior or you see a problem—your child's throwing food, not eating vegetables, sitting and watching TV or playing with the computer all day—and you can't fix it using the methods you already use, or when it looks as if these usual methods are not quite getting your child where you would like her to be. Sometimes you can screw a bolt on or off by hand and really do not need a wrench. Sometimes you need a wrench, and it's good to have one as backup. And so our toolkit.

An exercise (a quiz!)

In this chapter I provided a template for how to use the toolkit and what to do in what order. Then I applied the template to typical problems that come up at different ages. Now it's your turn. Here is a friendly set of quizlike prompts to help you design a behavior-change program. Fill in—write in—your answers to these as an exercise that will be a great start for you in developing effective programs to change behaviors you want to change. We will assume for this example that we are working with a young child, preschool through elementary-school age. Just fill in the blanks—if you have a real example, that's great (and my condolences), but making one up will still call on your newfound skills. (Heads up: I'm about to use some tried-and-true antecedents on you.) You can take the quiz or skip it, as you like (choice). I'm sure you'll do fine, but I don't expect any reader to get them all right (gentle challenge).

The behavior you want to change in your child is: (Give a brief statement here like "talking nicely to his sister more often.")

_____

If there's a behavior you want to decrease or eliminate, what is it, *and* what's the positive opposite you want to build up in its place? _____

_____

Now define in a little more detail what the good behavior would look like. (For example, if you could tell him what to say, what would he say to his sister?) _____

_____

_____

What would be a good prompt you could offer to increase the likelihood of the behavior? _____

_____

Are there any setting events that could be used to make it more likely that he would do the desired behavior? (For instance, is there a game or some other activity that he and his sister like or do well together that makes social interaction between them more cooperative?) _____

_____

_____

Does the behavior you want to see ever occur at all, or at the moment is it really zero and never? If the behavior occurs or if small pieces or approximations of the behavior occur, note here what they are and when they have occurred. Just one or two examples would be fine. _____

_____

_____

_____

If the child is only doing approximations of the desired behavior, we will want to use shaping. So here list some of the steps along the way from what the child does now (for example, says nice things once in a while) to what you would like him to do (say nice things almost all of the time). List steps along the way (such as saying nice things twice a day, then four times a day). _____

_____

_____

If the behavior never occurs or occurs rarely, what could you do? (If you need to go to a simulation game, what would the game be?) _____

_____

You will use praise as a main consequence to reinforce the behavior. Describe what that praise should be like. That is, for it to be effective, what three elements should it have?

- The tone of the praise should be _____ .
- When you praise, you should state exactly _____ .
- Then you should go over to the child and _____ .

You will use some punishment to address behavior you want to decrease, so whenever the child does it (for example, says something nasty to his sister), what will you do?

_____

_____

Keep in mind

Avoid blame (especially self-blame)

Be careful not to blame yourself for your child's undesirable behaviors. I mention this because I have seen many parents, especially mothers, who blame themselves for their children's serious problems (autism, for instance, or an eating disorder) and for the everyday challenges of the type we have been discussing (tantrums, nastiness, not listening, and so on). We know that human behavior is influenced by so many factors that it's usually impossible to isolate one as *the* cause. It's unlikely that you're the sole or even main cause of your child's misbehavior. Actually, in any given case you may have little or no role in the misbehavior at all. But behavior is malleable, which means that you can take the lead in changing your child's behavior for the better. So while you shouldn't waste energy on holding yourself responsible for undesirable behaviors you see in your child now, take heart in knowing that you *can* change those behaviors.

Model the behaviors you wish, provide the contextual influences we have discussed, and then apply the tools we illustrated. You'll be surprised by the results. Parents who work with us at the Yale Parenting Center are usually relieved to discover just how much they can change behavior, and they typically benefit from reduced stress in the home, better relationships among family members, and other such changes. But their strongest response is surprise that their children's behavior can be changed. In science, the ability of the brain to change is referred to as "plasticity." In developing new habits, new ways of responding in everyday situations, we can work directly on changing the brain, and this can happen over the entire life span. Remember the expression "You can't teach an old dog new tricks"? It's wrong. Just as your child can learn new behaviors and attitudes, you can learn how to change your child's behavior.

Just get through a tantrum

Let's say you have a program in place with your child to reduce or eliminate extreme tantrums. You're focusing on positive opposites and the program seems to be working. The extreme tantrums are down from two per day to two per week. Also, their length and severity are trending down. But the child still has the tantrums, and you've got a question: "What do I do when we're in the middle of the tantrum? There is no positive opposite to reinforce, no opportunity for praise. It's a total meltdown. Where and how do I use the ABCs?"

The program mostly happens when there *isn't* a tantrum going on, and we're confident that it will reduce and eventually eliminate extreme tantrums. There is much less one can do during a tantrum, but there are some things.

Perhaps the best analogy to a tantrum is a person who's drowning. You don't try to teach the person how to swim right then; you just do what you can to save her. Later, when she's not drowning, you can teach her how to swim, which is the positive opposite of drowning, and that will eventually decrease the likelihood of drowning.

So you are in the middle of a doozy of a tantrum. What to do? First, make sure everyone is safe—from crashing into the furniture, from being hit by a flying elbow or thrown objects. Do what you can to ensure safety.

Second, don't argue with your child, don't reason with him, don't do anything physical—like drag him to a different room or restrain him physically—unless it's absolutely necessary. Do not drag him to time out or otherwise try to punish him in the middle of the tantrum. Each of these is likely to increase the tantrum's magnitude and duration, and anything physical is likely to lead to side effects, the most common of which is you being hit. I have seen this happen enough times to know that a parent who gets hit in such a situation usually becomes furious and escalates whatever punishment he was using or thinking of using. Once you start increasing your involvement—more lecturing, more shouting, more physical touching, holding, restraining—the emotional side effects of punishment, the child's disruptive behavior, your stress, and your escalation of punishment all move fast in the wrong direction.

Third, as soon as you can safely walk away, do so, even if the child follows you. We *want* ignoring because the likelihood of attending to the tantrum will unwittingly reinforce tantrum behavior.

Fourth, as the tantrum winds down, is there any positive feature you have seen? Did the child calm down more quickly than usual, did he not swear this time, did he not throw anything this time? If there is something that clearly is better than usual as his tantrums go, praise that softly and gently. Do not make something up, but praise any conspicuous improvement in the nature of this tantrum compared to a previous or usual one.

Fifth, do not return to the tantrum as a discussion topic later with some moralizing or reflective lesson. "You know, that big explosive tantrum yesterday was not fun for anyone." Forget it. It's much better to invest your time and effort in reinforcing calm behavior and being able to handle any frustration, however major or minor.

The same general approach applies to other blowups, like a teenager flying into a rage or two siblings getting into a serious fight. Make sure everyone is safe, don't engage, walk away as soon as you can, reinforce any feature of the event that was an improvement over the usual, and don't keep harping on it. Just get through it. Then, when things have calmed down, go back to reinforcing positive opposites.

You can't punish the behavior away

As a parent you have the unique role of teaching your child what to do in the home, at school, in life. Punishment will not do that. But so much of what we want to change in our children is about eliminating or reducing irritating behavior, and that tends to lead to punishment. No matter how much I have noted that punishment is not an effective procedure for changing behavior, it will be difficult to avoid.

There are strong forces that help maintain our use of ineffective punishment. First, there is the punishment trap I discussed in chapter four: the immediate cessation of the negative behavior after we shout, scream, or hit maintains our use of those punishment practices even though beyond that moment the actual frequency of the behavior we punished does not change. Second, researchers have learned recently that aggressive behavior activates and stimulates reward centers in the human brain, and punishing a child is aggressive behavior. The act of punishing looks as if it has effects in the brain similar to those caused by the use of an illicit drug. That surge of feeling qualifies as a reward—it feels good—which means that for many parents just punishing the child to get rid of behavior will be maintained by its own internal reward, even if it patently doesn't work. Third, there's another kind of reward, a sense of satisfaction, in feeling that you have done something about the problem of your child's misbehavior. And if you think it was the "right" thing to do, morally, that only increases your satisfaction.

I do not expect to overcome all of these attractions of punishment. And, as I have discussed, merely explaining the severe limitations of punishment will not do much to sway anyone. Even if you're convinced, understanding by itself is a weak influence on behavior. If you say to someone at a restaurant, "You know that the Double Chocolate Mud Mountain in front of you right now has enough calories to feed a family of sixteen for a day," that person is likely to say, "Yeah, I know," and then smile and eat it.

The way to overcome the pull of punishment is to use methods that work better. Use positive opposites to develop behavior and you'll see a lot more success. That doesn't mean that you should never punish. Mild, brief punishment doesn't do much harm, and it can help. But keep the proportions sound: a lot of positive reinforcement, a little punishment.

A check on yourself: if you are consistently punishing a given behavior, you need to begin a positive-opposite program instead. Now try to, and arrange to, catch the child being good—engaging in the positive opposite. How often? There is no scientifically tested answer, but make sure there are many more opportunities to reinforce positive opposites than to punish the undesired behavior.

Age- and stage-related behaviors

So many of the challenging behaviors children present are age- or stage-related. By that I mean they come on fairly predictably and also go away. Among these are thumb sucking, clumsiness (dropping glasses, spilling), interrupting, having toileting accidents after you thought the child was fully toilet trained, lying, disagreeing with you no matter what you say, showing off, not paying attention at school, talking too much or too little, teen attitude, and more.

In general, these behaviors have several characteristics in common. They are so intensely annoying that you want to sue the hospital for not telling you about them when you and your infant were discharged after your delivery. You did not do anything to deserve them and you shouldn't have to put up with them. And when these behaviors have a victim or target, you are the one wearing the bull's-eye T-shirt, and you're also the cleanup maintenance staff who has to deal with any messes they cause.

These behaviors vary markedly among children. If you have more than one child, they probably won't show the same behaviors. Some children show a lot of them, and others show none or almost none. This plays with your mind. You find yourself engaging in a depressing internal monologue. "Why is this child so high on the rotten scale? Is it because of something I did? Why does my own child hate me? I don't deserve this. This child is totally out of control. Can parents run away from home?"

Some of these behaviors are part of development, and here are a few things to keep in mind:

1. The behavior is likely to go away by itself or in the course of your usual parenting. This can be said confidently because there are very few teenagers who are still having toileting accidents or sucking their thumbs.
2. You need to make a decision as to whether the behavior is tolerable, whether you can wait it out or not. This is all a matter of degree and personal choice, affected by the level of intensity in the behavior of your child and by your own tolerance level.
3. Is the behavior interfering with functioning? If the child is in trouble at school, a sibling in the home is made very anxious or disturbed by the behavior, or family relations are significantly interfered with in some other way, these are good reasons to intervene. Start with the toolkit this book provides. If the behavior is very extreme, you may want to call on professional help.

Conclusion

So now you've got a toolkit full of tools, and instructions about how to use them properly. You may well be excited to give it all a try, and you may also be worrying, like a person embarking on a new diet, that you'll find it hard to follow through. Bear a couple of things in mind as you go forward.

First, the programs do not require perfection, but the more carefully you carry out the procedures, the more likely you will see behavior change and the sooner you can stop a program completely.

Second, any particular program is likely to be fairly short-lived.

The typical period of a program to, say, eliminate tantrums or build better homework habits is a few weeks. So don't think of embarking on a program as a lifelong commitment to praising homework-doing every single time you see it. Yes, you'll want to be on it as much as possible for a couple of weeks, perhaps even as much as a month, but then you'll fade back to a regular level of parental interest and involvement. And, in fact, if the program has gone well, you'll be able to be a lot less involved in getting your child to do his homework because he'll be doing it on his own (one of the things you were reinforcing in the program), and you won't be nagging him about it and checking up on him all the time.

So you don't have to be perfect, and you won't be doing any program indefinitely. When you identify a behavior you want to see more or less of, you'll plan the appropriate program, do it as intensely as you can for a brief period, then fade it out and move on.

You have worked so hard to raise your child. The effort and commitment on your part began immediately at birth—probably well before birth, in fact. You have ambitions and goals for your child—and also some frustrations, because sometimes it seems that your child is the only person in the household who is not cooperating in the heroic effort to give him or her a better life. The tools you've been mastering in this book are not mere techniques to eliminate an annoying behavior here or there. That's never the goal of child rearing. We want to help our children develop as individuals who can function well in what they do and have skills and aptitudes that will make their lives more rewarding for themselves and for others. The toolkit can help you build behaviors and, through that, larger habits and traits of character you want your child to have. They're not just tools to fix a leak here and there; they're tools to help build a good life for your family, now and well into the future.

Notes

Introduction

vii *The body of good research:* In this book I draw on a great deal of research, in keeping with my intent to bring you the practical benefits of the best scientific work on parenting and child rearing. Occasionally I will identify the source when I make a specific claim based on a specific study, but if you wish to go more deeply into the research, much of it is cited in a more technical text: A. E. Kazdin, *Behavior Modification in Applied Settings,* 7th ed. (Long Grove, IL: Waveland Press, 2013).

viii *There are also more single parents:* Source: E. Wildsmith, N. R. Steward-Streng, and J. Manlove, "Childbearing Outside of Marriage: Estimates and Trends in the United States," *Child Research Brief* (November 2011), Publication #201129 4301, Washington, DC (http://www.childtrends.org/Files/Child_Trends-2011_11_01_RB_NonmaritalCB.pdf).

1. Laying the Groundwork for Good Behavior

11 *A team of researchers:* Source: J. J. McComas, D. P. Wacker, and L. J. Cooper, "Increasing Compliance with Medical Procedures: Application of the High-Probability Behavior Request Procedure to a Toddler," *Journal of Applied Behavior Analysis* 31 (1998): 287–90.

2. What You Want to Change

42 *Another example is a project:* Source: R. G. Miltenberger, C. Flessner, B. Gatheridge, B. Johnson, M. Satterlund, and K. Egemo, "Evaluation of

Behavioral Skills Training to Prevent Gun Play in Children," *Journal of Applied Behavior Analysis* 37 (2004): 513–16.

4. Decreasing Misbehavior

104 *Withholding reinforcement was also used:* Source: K. G. France and S. M. Hudson, "Behavior Management of Infant Sleep Disturbance," *Journal of Applied Behavior Analysis* 23 (1990): 91–98.

5. The Routines of Family Life

136 *Are the behavior problems caused:* Sources: S. C. J. Huijbregts, J. R. Séguin, M. Zoccolillo, M. Boivin, and R. E. Tremblay, "Maternal Prenatal Smoking, Parental Antisocial Behavior, and Early Childhood Physical Aggression," *Developmental Psychopathology* 20 (2008): 437–53. M. Weitzman, S. Gortmaker, and A. Sobol, "Maternal Smoking and Behavior Problems of Children," *Pediatrics* 90 (1992): 342–49.

Additional Resources

Visit our websites

Yale Parenting Center: http://childconductclinic.yale.edu
Press and interviews: http://www.alankazdin.com

Additional readings by the authors on
parenting in everyday situations

"Tiny Tyrants: How to Really Change Your Kid's Behavior" http://www.slate.com/id/2188744/.

"Family Feuds: How to Make 'Timeouts' Less Like Bar Fights" http://www.slate.com/id/2194331/.

"Spare the Rod: Why You Shouldn't Hit Your Kids" http://www.slate.com/id/2200450/.

"Why Can't Johnny Jump Tall Buildings? Parents Expect Way Too Much From Their Kids" http://www.slate.com/id/2204113.

"Reading Isn't Fundamental: How to Help Your Child Learn to Read" http://www.slate.com/id/2206105/.

"Your Kids Will Imitate You: Use It as a Force for Good" http://www.slate.com/id/2209882/.

"No, You Shut Up! What to Do When Your Kid Provokes You Into an Inhuman Rage" http://www.slate.com/id/2210616/.

"The Messy Room Dilemma: When to Ignore Behavior, When to Change It" http://www.slate.com/id/2214678/.

"I Think I'm Worried About My Kid" http://www.slate.com/id/2218374/.

"Bullies: They Can Be Stopped, but It Takes a Village" http://www.slate.com/id/2223976/.

"Plan B: What to Do When All Else Has Failed to Change Your Kid's Behavior" http://www.slate.com/id/2228559/.

"Like a Rat: Animal Research and Your Child's Behavior" http://www.slate.com/id/2234707/.

"No Brakes! Part I: Risk and the Adolescent Brain" http://www.slate.com/id/2243435/.

"No Brakes! Part II: The Best Way to Guide Your Teenager Through the High-Risk Years" http://www.slate.com/id/2243436/.

"If You're Good, I'll Buy You a Toy: The Difference Between Bribing Your Child and Rewarding Your Child" http://www.slate.com/id/2248766.

"Get Off Facebook and Do Something! How to Motivate an Inert Child" http://www.slate.com/id/2254448/.

"Children and Stress: The New Science on Chronically Harsh and Conflict-Ridden Households" http://www.slate.com/id/2262309/.

Index